MERCEDES-BENZ V8s

Limousines, saloons, sedans. 1963 to date

Osprey AutoHistory

MERCEDES- BENZ V8s

Limousines, saloons, sedans. 1963 to date

F. WILSON McCOMB

Published in 1980 by Osprey Publishing Limited,
12–14 Long Acre; London WC2 9LP
Member company of the George Philip Group

United States distribution by

Osceola, Wisconsin 54020, USA

British Library Cataloguing in Publication Data

McComb, Frederick Wilson
    Mercedes-Benz V8s.
    (Osprey autohistory).
    1. Mercedes automobile
    I. Title
629.22′22   TL215.M4/
ISBN 0-85045-383-6

Editor Tim Parker
Associate Michael Sedgwick
Photography Mirco Decet
Design Fred Price

Filmset and printed in England by
BAS Printers Limited, Over Wallop, Hampshire

Contents

Author's acknowledgements
6

Chapter 1
The mystique of Mercedes-Benz
8

Chapter 2
The first V8
21

Chapter 3
6·3-litres
30

Chapter 4
3·5- and 4·5-litres
55

Chapter 5
6·9-litres
84

Chapter 6
3·8- and 5·0-litres
96

Specifications
113

Photographic acknowledgements
133

Index
134

Author's Ackowledgements

It is a source of increasing embarrassment to discover, with each new book, how little one really seems to know about *anything*—and no great consolation to realize one is not necessarily alone in that plight. This time, however, my thanks and acknowledgements are perhaps more heartfelt than usual.

I address them first to Erik Johnson and Marlies Salmon of Mercedes-Benz (United Kingdom) Ltd., and their colleagues in Germany, Günther Molter and Bernd Harling. Other members of Daimler-Benz AG who provided immense assistance were Professor Breitschwerdt and Professor Förster, Hans-Otto Derndinger, Guntram Huber, Karl Kollmann and Rolf Ohlendorf. Among Mercedes-Benz retailers in Britain, Owen Williams and Tony Bird (Woking Motors Ltd.), Adrian Hamilton (Duncan Hamilton Ltd.), and Huck Hale and John Young (Rose & Young Ltd.) all went out of their way to help me. Valued assistance came also from Peter Brockes of the National Motor Museum Library at Beaulieu, Glass's Guide Service Ltd., from Rex Greenslade, Bill Mason, Cyril Posthumus, and from Andrew Rodger of Robert Bosch Ltd. Last but (we have agreed) not least among the personalities is my editor, Tim Parker, the extent of whose contribution I shall probably never admit.

The periodicals referred to most were *Autocar, Automobile Quarterly, Car, Motor, Motor Sport* and *Road & Track*. In addition to Nick Georgano's ever-useful *Complete Encyclopaedia of the Motor Car* and *Encyclopaedia of Motor Sport*, I consulted *A Racing Motorist*, by Rudolf Caracciola, *Continental Sports Cars*, by William Boddy, *The Grand Prix Car 1906/1939*, by Laurence Pomeroy, *Grand Prix Driver*, by Hermann Lang, *Motoring My Way*, by Stanley Sedgwick, *Motor Racing with Mercedes-Benz*, by George Monkhouse, *Speed Was My Life*, by Alfred Neubauer, and *The Thoroughbred Motor-car 1930/1940*, by David Scott-Moncrieff. In a special category all by itself I place *The Mercedes-Benz Racing Cars*, by Karl Ludvigsen, whose scholarly return to primary sources in 1971 exploded many long-cherished myths. If Karl had researched and written the history of Mercedes-Benz production cars with equal skill, the rest of us would indeed be out of business.

F. W. McC.

Chapter 1
The mystique of Mercedes~Benz

Last summer one of those rugged, diesel-engined Mercedes saloons pulled into my front drive, and out stepped an Austrian holidaymaker who had come to collect from me a decayed Frogeye Sprite. How this came about would take too long to explain; suffice it to say that it did. With a borrowed hacksaw my visitor cut the Sprite in two at its door-openings, and then he proceeded to heave the entire tail section (which was what he really wanted) into the luggage compartment of the Mercedes. As jagged edges of British steel gouged through German paintwork and trim I ventured to protest about the damage he was doing to his own car. The Austrian shrugged his shoulders and said unconcernedly: 'Why worry? It is only a taxi.'

At the time of this occurrence, my blood pressure had scarcely returned to normal after road-testing the magnificent 450 SEL 6·9-litre saloon a few weeks earlier, so it was interesting to be reminded that however awe-inspiring some of Daimler-Benz AG's products may be, many of them have long been 'only a taxi' to the inhabitants of Continental Europe and, indeed, remain so to this day. Later in the year I tested a new model so utterly lacking in performance that normal overtaking became a hazardous venture, and to me its sole virtue seemed to be that high-quality construction and apparent inde-structibility which makes the Mercedes so attractive to taxi operators.

Not that the combination of reliability and longevity is altogether scorned by other buyers, of course. Recently one of Britain's leading Mercedes-Benz distributors talked to me of the days when a customer could literally buy two Jaguars for the price of one Mercedes. This obviously made the German car difficult to sell in the UK—but not impossible, by any means. My informant admitted defeat, though, in the case of a fellow-member of his local golf club who flatly refused to buy a Mercedes. This splendid patriot actually *did* buy his Jaguars two at a time, so that he could count on always having one in working order.

Mercedes is, beyond all argument, one of the great names of motoring history, its past an intrinsic part of its mystique. To many people a Mercedes-Benz will always be a 'Big Merc' (except in the USA, where a Merc is in fact a Ford Mercury, and therefore essentially a domestic product). One sees an imaginary SSKL, bold as Bismarck, and hears the banshee wail of its clutch-engaged supercharger. There is a mental picture of massive limousines, the choice of emperors, czars and maharajahs for the most prestigious cer-emonial occasions. One thinks of Caracciola, Lang and von Brauchitsch in motor racing's heroic days, as they fought to control the most powerful Grand Prix cars ever built. It is impossible to dismiss these associations, and if one could, one would no longer have a full understanding of the marque's endur-ing reputation.

The problem is, however, that mystique lies perilously close to mythology. The sports/racing

Developed as a sports/racer, the SSKL had a 7·1-litre six-cylinder engine which produced 170 bhp unblown or 300 with the clutch-engaged supercharger in action. Its successes included the 1931 Mille Miglia, Eifelrennen, German GP and Avusrennen

SSKL was indeed one of the most exciting vehicles (some would call it *the* most exciting) that ever turned a wheel, and from end to end it looked that way. But its claim to greatness is surely invalidated by the near-impossibility of keeping it pointing in the right direction at high speed (unless one's name was Rudi Caracciola). Contrariwise, the 500K and later 540K were assuredly very comfortable and relaxing to drive, and they also looked magnificent if you like that sort of thing—an auction price of almost half-a-million dollars suggests that if you do like it, you will apparently like it a lot. But their actual performance on the road fell far short of the promise held out by their appearance, and as T. S. Eliot almost said, it is our business as honest men not to assume that what some people like is what we all ought to like.

My point is that the very prestige of Mercedes-Benz may cause us to admire the marque for the wrong reasons. The now somewhat exaggerated renown of the pre-war Mercedes-Benz leads some pundits to believe that the Stuttgart-Unterturkheim products of that era were far better cars than those of today, whereas I would suggest the exact opposite is nearer the truth. Men who know their business have described certain recent models as the best-engineered, the best-built, the most advanced, in fact the nearest approach to complete perfection that has yet been achieved. My own view is that although some Mercedes-Benzes are and always have been ponderously conservative vehicles, the V8-engined cars in particular have long been a cut above the rest, and sometimes head and shoulders above the equivalent models built by rival manufacturers.

Almost half-a-million dollars was paid for a model 500K with 2-seater roadster bodywork, of the type also seen on this 1936 model 540K, at an auction in California early in 1979

11

Above *Karl Benz (1844–1929) built his first car in 1885, sold his first two years later, and became the world's first automobile manufacturer. He was the son of a railway engine driver*

Centre *Gottlieb Daimler (1834–1900), son of a baker, built the world's first high-speed internal combustion engine in 1883, and his first experimental car in 1886*

Right *Wilhelm Maybach (1844–1929) was Daimler's partner in the engineering business they started near Stuttgart in 1882, and did most of the design work. Their first production car was exhibited at Paris in 1889*

The Mercedes owes its existence to the demand made eight decades ago for an automobile that would combine ultimate performance with passenger safety and high-quality construction. But the history of its forebears is as old as the motor industry itself. Daimler-Benz AG are entitled to call themselves the world's oldest automobile manufacturers because Karl Benz was the first to build and sell motor vehicles on a regular production basis, and Gottlieb Daimler (with his partner, Wilhelm Maybach) was the first to develop a petrol engine of the type best suited to their propulsion. The name of Mercedes came into the picture some fifteen years later, at the turn of the century, when Emile Jellinek of Nice ordered from the Cannstatt Daimler factory a series of fast cars with better handling qualities than those of the existing 24 hp Daimler Phoenix, whose stability had already proved very doubtful in speed events. The model that was built at Jellinek's request incorporated some features which were completely new to the motoring world, and some already known to pioneer car-makers but not previously combined in one vehicle. Inlet valves that were operated mechani-

Far left *Emile Jellinek, Austro-Hungarian diplomat and entrepreneur, persuaded the Daimler company to build faster and better cars which he raced and sold to the wealthy residents of Nice*

Left *Mercédès Jellinek, whose father used her name as his own pseudonym when racing, and adopted it for the new-style Daimlers he drove and sold from 1901 onwards*

cally, instead of merely being sucked open as the pistons descended, combined with better throttle and induction arrangements to improve the driver's control over engine speed, and this together with a scroll clutch and visible lever 'gate' allowed him to make faster gear-changes. The new and more efficient 'honeycomb' radiator, with its multitude of small tubes to improve heat dissipation, reduced the capacity (and therefore the weight) of the cooling system, which also helped to lower the bonnet line. The entire car was at once lower, longer and lighter than its predecessors, and showed its paces with a string of successes at the Nice Speed Week of 1901. They were quickly followed by equally sweeping commercial success when cars of this type were marketed as 'Mercédès', the name of Jellinek's 10-year-old daughter and the pseudonym that he himself had adopted when racing.

It has been said that anti-German feeling in France persuaded the Daimler Company to adopt a different name there, but it is scarcely irrelevant that Panhard & Levassor, who had fitted Daimler engines to their own cars for many years, still held certain marketing rights in that country. What-

13

ever the reason, Jellinek (now one of the Directors of the Daimler Company) secured exclusive rights to sell the cars under the name of his choice in France, Belgium, his native Austro-Hungary and the USA. Elsewhere they were simply the 'New Daimler', and when reference was made to Mercedes in Germany, the French-style accents were omitted. With or without accents, however, the name of Mercedes was from the start associated with that most desirable attribute, outstanding performance that could be safely enjoyed by the discerning motorist.

The successes at Nice served as a mere curtain-raiser to frequent racing victories elsewhere, of which the most notable was Jenatzy's win in the 1903 Gordon Bennett Trophy race with a 60 hp touring model. The following year, William K. Vanderbilt and Baron de Caters both drove Mercedes to raise the Land Speed Record, although they both failed by a narrow margin to achieve the first 100 mph. That figure was soon within the grasp of Mercedes, however, and when attention turned to Grand Prix racing shortly after, the factory had a new contender ready to take the honours at Dieppe in 1908.

The rival factory of Benz, meanwhile, had at first earned a less enviable reputation for building vehicles that were reliable, but rather slow and old-fashioned in design. Then a change of policy at Mannheim brought more up-to-date models, and several sporting successes were gained from 1906 onwards. When Mercedes won the 1908 French Grand Prix, two racing Benzes occupied second and third places at the finish of that supremely important event. That same year Benz won the race from St Petersburg to Moscow, and in America further Benz victories were gained by Bruce-Brown, the flamboyant Barney Oldfield and others, the climax being a fantastic Daytona

Beach run at more than 140 mph by Bob Burman in 1911, using the renowned 21-litre Blitzen Benz. As Karl Ludvigsen has pointed out in his splendid history of Mercedes-Benz racing, this speed was far in excess of the highest then attained by any car, train or aeroplane, allowing Benz publicity men to make the simple and unqualified statement that 'Only a bullet has travelled faster'. In a decade, Mannheim had progressed a long way

Victor Hémery and mechanic change tyres during the 1908 French GP at the world's first 'pits' (a trench in front of the grandstand). Their Benz came second to Lautenschlager's Mercedes

from the outdated designs that almost put Benz out of business.

There were many more such achievements by the two separate marques prior to their amalgamation in 1926. The year after, this union of the two oldest names in motoring history was fittingly celebrated at the new Nürburgring circuit, when three Model S Mercedes-Benz sports cars, built by Daimler-Benz AG, scored a convincing 1-2-3 victory in the German Grand Prix.

The extent to which bread-and-butter passenger cars benefit from racing development is a classic saloon-bar subject, hotly and inconclusively debated by motoring enthusiasts since one horseless carriage first went chuffing past another. Of the multitude of racing successes that Mercedes-Benz has recorded over the years, many served to demonstrate some technical innovation that would subsequently be incorporated in production cars, but it has not always been so; indeed, the racing department has been known to borrow from the production line to achieve better results. Jellinek's 1901 Mercedes, however, was designed specifically to satisfy the requirements of an ambitious amateur racing driver. Moreover, it was the embodiment of what is now known at Stuttgart as 'co-ordinated integration', defined by Daimler-Benz as 'the thorough development of individual components and their integration into a balanced overall concept'. Or in somewhat less stilted language, 'getting it all together'.

This is a process that can take some time, and possibly accounts for a few of the inconsistencies that turn Mercedes-Benz history into such a curious mixture of daringly advanced technology and stuffily conservative design. It seems so odd that a production Mercedes could be bought with front-wheel brakes in 1903, twenty years before their adoption by most manufacturers, but

Mercedes-Benz were the last to build cars with wooden wheels—in 1939! Only Mercedes could still be found using chain-driven Grand Prix cars in 1913, but the first rear-engined Grand Prix car was the Benz Tropfenwagen of 1923. The first Grand Prix winner with all-independent suspension was a Mercedes-Benz (1934), as was the first with inboard brakes or desmodromic valve operation (1954), not to mention the first air-brake-equipped sports-racing car (1955). But some people still consider Daimler-Benz unduly resistant to change, citing as evidence the shape of the production cars. However, a moment's consideration of the technical specification—or merely of the aerodynamic drag factor!—reveals this to be a very superficial judgment.

The policy of gradual change may also explain the mind-blowing confusion of Mercedes-Benz model designations. In theory it makes perfectly good sense. The number is supposed to indicate the capacity: 200 for 2·0 litres, 220 for 2·2 litres, 230 for 2·3 litres and so on—which is all very well until we come across a 2778 cc Model 250, a 6332 cc Model 300 or a 6834 cc Model 450. We are told that D stands for Diesel, DS for Special (*Speziell*), S for Sport, SS for Super Sport, L for Light (*Leicht*), K for Short (*Kurz*), E for Injection (*Einspritzung*), and so on. In practice, unfortunately, it immediately becomes obvious that the alphabetical designations frequently mean something entirely different. Sometimes K means Supercharged (*Kompressor*) instead of Short. Sometimes L doesn't mean Light but Long (*Lange*), in which case the car is actually heavier than the short-wheelbase version, and especially if it really means Luxury (*Luxus*) instead of either Short or Long. Similarly, the etymology of the word Coupé demands its application to a shortened or close-coupled vehicle, but Mercedes-

Benz will apply it to a *lengthened* version of a model that began life as a short-wheelbase car. As for the S designation, this is now applied so all-embracingly that it obviously no longer means Sport, but the theory that it denotes either the New S series (of September 1972) or the *new* New S series (of September 1979) doesn't hold water because its use precedes the introduction of either.

Like many car manufacturers Mercedes-Benz, in pre-Hitler days, would quote a fiscal horse-power rating followed by maximum engine bhp (8/38, 12/55, etc.), with a three-part designation for supercharged models to indicate the fiscal horse-power, output unblown, and output with blower engaged. Thus the production version of the SSK was also referred to as the 27/170/225, but in Britain a different taxation system plus a mysteriously increased bhp figure turned the same car into the 38/250. After 1933 the fiscal rating was usually dropped in Germany, giving a somewhat confusing 100/160 for the 500K, for example. There were sometimes model names like 'Stuttgart' or 'Mannheim' which indicated where the car was built, except in certain cases ('Nürburgring', for example,) when they obviously did not.

Largest of all pre-war Mercedes-Benzes was the mighty *Grosser*, variously translatable as Great, Super or just plain Big, and powered by a 7655 cc (95 × 135 mm) straight-eight engine with ohv, dual ignition, and the usual clutch-engaged supercharger. When introduced in 1930, the Grosser had a simple rigid-axle chassis, and the engine gave 150 bhp unsupercharged or 200 bhp supercharged. In 1938 this was succeeded by a new model with a chassis very similar to that used for the contemporary Grand Prix cars. The frame was made up of oval tubes, the front suspension was independent by coil springs and wishbones, and the rear suspension was of the de Dion type, often

Top *The first Grosser Mercedes-Benz, introduced in 1930, had rigid axles and a 7.7-litre engine, supplied with or without supercharger*

Below *Biggest of prewar Mercedes-Benz models, the 1938 Grosser featured a chassis similar to the contemporary GP cars. The right front seat of the open touring car converted into a raised platform, where such notabilities as Adolf Hitler would stand during a parade*

mistakenly called independent. Oddly enough, much of the reference material published by Daimler-Benz AG states that the car had independent suspension all round, the rear of swing-axle design, but this is not so.

The engine's many refinements included sodium-cooled valves, roller tappets, three oil-pumps, and nine main bearings (like the crank-shaft, the camshaft also had nine bearings). There were servo-assisted hydraulic brakes, and a five-speed synchromesh gearbox with overdrive top, while the total fuel tankage (including reserve) was forty-seven gallons—and all of it needed, with a consumption of around 9 mpg. Depending on the type of coachwork fitted, the Grosser turned the scales at about 8000 lb and was at least 20 ft long, but maximum speed was something over 105 mph, engine power output having increased to 155 bhp unsupercharged, and 230 bhp with the supercharger engaged. When this was done, said *The Motor* road-tester, 'the characteristic Mercedes scream bursts out into full song, and the effect on loiterers holding the crown of the road is electric.'

The same magazine remarked that on the 12 ft 8 in wheelbase it was no problem to mount bodywork big enough for eight or nine passengers, which must have been an impressive sight indeed. However, the Grosser is usually associated with heads of State who bought the car as personal transport for grand occasions, and the *Offener Tourenwagen* or Open Touring Car had a special front seat that converted into a raised platform, on which an important somebody might stand during a parade to acknowledge the acclaim of his people. One has only to close one's eyes for a moment to see Adolf Hitler doing exactly that in a Grosser Mercedes, as he did many times during his career as the German Führer.

Naturally, production of this ultimate Mercedes-Benz ceased on the outbreak of war in 1939, and almost a quarter of a century passed before Stuttgart announced the new Grosser, or model 600. It was revealed as a superb creation, not merely luxurious but highly advanced in its technical specification, and in every way a most worthy successor to the pre-war Grosser. The interest that it aroused in the motoring Press was heightened by the fact that Stuttgart had, for the first time, chosen a V8 engine to power a production Mercedes-Benz.

It was not, however, the first V8-engined Mercedes-Benz of all time. That distinction belongs to model W.165, a single-seater racing car that did almost as much to enhance the marque's reputation as its wellnigh unbeatable stable-mates of the pre-war Grand Prix era, although it competed in one race, and one only.

Chapter 2
The first V8

The first Mercedes-Benz V8 engine was born of the personal rivalry that existed between Adolf Hitler and Benito Mussolini. In the late Twenties, although clouds of latter-day nostalgia now tend to obscure the fact, Grand Prix racing was at a low ebb. One AIACR formula after another was rejected, the participants throwing away the rulebook to organize major races as free-formula or sports car events. In this situation, France did most of the winning at first with the beautiful Type 35B Bugatti, leaving only an occasional crumb for Germany's SSK Mercedes-Benz. Then, however, *Il Duce* made it clear to the car-builders of Italy that he expected them to win in future, for the greater glory of the *Fascisti*. And it was so, the lean and lovely P3 Alfa-Romeo taking most of the Grands Prix in 1932, with strong support from Maserati in 1933.

All that Daimler-Benz could do initially was to trim some 250 lb off the rather Wagnerian SSK, and in the fearless hands of Caracciola the SSKL was not to be ignored. But it was still essentially a sports car, and very outdated by the time it was revealed that a new maximum-weight GP formula would apply from the beginning of 1934. This seemed to put Germany completely out of the running—until Hitler, the new German Chancellor, announced that the manufacturer who restored the prestige of the Fatherland by building race-winning cars would enjoy a substantial government subsidy, plus favourable consideration for armament contracts.

The result is history: Daimler-Benz and the new Auto Union organization designed and built a series of single-seaters that achieved total supremacy in motor racing. Of sixty-six major events held between 1934 and 1939, fifty-six were won by a German car—thirty-four by Mercedes-Benz, and twenty-two by Auto Union. As for the Italians, they had to suffer the special humiliation of seeing the Italian Grand Prix won by Germany five times running. It was more than they could stomach. Just after the fifth such defeat, at Monza in September 1938, the head of the Italian motor sporting organization announced that the next major Grand Prix in their calendar, the Tripoli GP of May 1939, would be confined to cars of only 1·5 litres. The internationally agreed limit at that time being three litres, this would exclude the current German racing cars altogether. It was naturally assumed that in eight months neither Auto Union nor Mercedes-Benz could design and build a completely new car capable of winning the race.

Four days later, at an emergency meeting at Untertürkheim, it was agreed that Daimler-Benz would meet the challenge by building a new model codenamed W.165 (W = *Wagen*). It was to be a scaled-down version of the existing W.154 3-litre model, using similar components (wherever this could be done successfully) in order to save every possible minute of design time. Development time, however, was a luxury they would have to forgo.

In halving the capacity of the larger car, Mercedes decided on a V8 configuration, which would make the engine shorter than a straight-eight of the same capacity, and maintain some useful similarities to the existing GP engine,

The first V8 Mercedes-Benz engine, a 1·5-litre designed in less than eight months. After the 1939 Tripoli GP it was converted to two-stage supercharging, as shown here

which was a V12. As near-identical valve gear was to be used, they chose a bore diameter of 64 mm, not much smaller than the 67 mm of the bigger unit, which meant that with a swept volume of 1495 cc, the new engine would have a piston stroke of only 58 mm. Nowadays widely recognized as more efficient, the 'oversquare' engine (with bore greater than stroke) was a considerable rarity before World War Two.

The 3-litre M.154 engine (M = *Motor*) had a Silumin crankcase containing a one-piece crankshaft, which revolved in seven roller bearings. The big-end bearings, too, were of roller type, and the connecting rods were forged in nickel-chrome steel. The chrome-steel cylinders were made individually, with integral cylinder heads, then welded together in groups of three on a common baseplate with their sheet-steel water jackets and

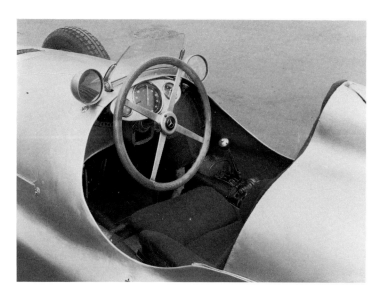

ports, two of these groups making up each bank of six cylinders in the 90-degree V12. There were four valves per cylinder (the hollow exhaust valves mercury-filled for cooling), and two gear-driven camshafts to each cylinder bank. There were also two superchargers, with a common carburettor on the suction side, but as these were run in parallel they gave only a single-stage boost. Dry-sump lubrication helped to keep engine height down, so as to achieve a low bonnet-line.

In general, the design of the 1·5-litre M.165 engine followed closely that of the 3-litre power unit: the light-alloy crankcase with cylinder banks at 90 degrees to each other; individual cylinders assembled in groups (but naturally in fours, not threes, for the V8); four overhead camshafts; mercury-cooled exhaust valves; dry-sump lubrication; ignition by single Bosch magneto, and so on. The shorter crankshaft of the V8 engine ran in five main bearings, not seven, and there were several detail differences in bottom-end design. When eventually tested with single-stage supercharging, the new small engine gave a power output of 256 bhp at 8000 rpm. This represents a *specific* output of 171·24 bhp per litre, making the M.165 proportionately more powerful *than any automobile engine Stuttgart ever made.* The bhp/litre figure is higher than that of the stupendously powerful 5·66-litre GP cars of 1937, or the 3-litre GP cars of 1938/9, or the 1938 5·5-litre record car—or, indeed, of the highly successful postwar 2·5-litre GP cars.

The chassis of the new small racing car was also modelled closely on the proven design of the larger machines. The frame was built up in the same way with side-members in thin-walled oval tubes, light but immensely strong. The rear suspension followed the same de Dion arrangement, with fore-and-aft torsion bars as the springing medium. The independent front suspension was again by coil springs and wishbones, but the W.165 chassis used the hydraulic shock-absorber arms as its upper front suspension members, instead of having the double wishbones of the W.154. The transmission layout, too, was similar, with a five-speed manually-controlled gearbox, offset driveline and ZF limited-slip differential. However, from sheer lack of space (the main frame members being only two feet apart) the driver's seat of the smaller car had to be offset to the opposite side to clear the driveline. At a fraction over 8 ft, the wheelbase was that of an Austin Allegro, and almost a foot less than the wheelbase of the 3-litre cars. The track was also reduced, front and rear, and at 1580 lb, the dry weight was down by almost 400 lb.

The W.165 project had first been discussed in mid-September 1938. Official authorization to build the cars came in mid-November, by which time many of the drawings had already been

One-time test driver for Austro-Daimler, Alfred Neubauer joined Mercedes in 1923, and served as the inimitable racing manager of Mercedes-Benz from 1926 until 1955

completed. By mid-February 1939 the last of the drawings had been done. Meanwhile the Mercedes racing department had also been continuing their development of the existing 3-litre cars, which made a triumphant debut with new bodywork at the Pau GP on April 2. A few days later, Rudi Caracciola and Hermann Lang were told to present themselves at the Hockenheim circuit, then used only for motorcycle events. The first complete W.165 Mercedes-Benz was ready for initial testing.

Both drivers were delighted with the new baby. Clothed in identical bodywork to that used at Pau, the 1·5-litre racing car did indeed look like an offspring of the big ones, as Caracciola later remarked. 'The same shape, the same bonnet. Graceful, like toys, and so low that when I stood up, my fingertips just touched them'. Lang was even more pleased, 'How the little tough guy accelerated! I took the car seriously, and drove it as this little masterpiece demanded to be driven'.

There was time to build only two cars for the Tripoli GP in May, and Stuttgart hedged their bets by building the two to slightly different specifications. The most significant difference was that Lang's car was geared high, for maximum speed, and Caracciola's slightly lower, for better acceleration. The plan evolved by Neubauer, the Team Manager, was that Lang should drive hard from the fall of the flag in an attempt to wreck the opposition, which consisted of no less than twenty-eight Italian cars. If his W.165 succumbed in the process, Caracciola could take up the challenge from there. Because of the very real danger of throwing a tread when driving at such speed on the sun-baked Tripoli road surface, Lang's car was also fitted with part-worn tyres, so as to reduce the centrifugal loading. It would therefore need a wheel-change at the refuelling stop, whereas Caracciola's car could start with full-tread tyres that would last the race, and make a much shorter pit-stop for fuel only.

The accounts of the race later given by Neubauer, Lang and Caracciola are somewhat conflicting, but it is clear that before the start there was considerable disagreement between the two drivers, each believing he had been given a raw deal. Lang, the ex-mechanic who had earned a place behind the wheel, desperately wanted to win at Tripoli for his third successive year. Caracciola, the popular hero who had long been acknowledged the team's Number One, was becoming uncomfortably aware of his rival's everincreasing skill, and deeply resented being given the slower car at this very fast circuit. Although theoretically their chances were even, Lang won at an average speed of 122·91 mph and almost lapped Caracciola, who finished second. Caracciola afterwards claimed he would have won, but the mechanics, he said, bungled his pit-stop. Lang

Hermann Lang, former racing mechanic, drove for the Mercedes-Benz racing team from 1935 to 1954 and won the Tripoli GP in 1937, 1938 and 1939

For years the unchallenged leader of the Mercedes-Benz team, Rudi Caracciola had to take second place to Lang when they both drove W.165 single-seaters in the 1939 Tripoli GP, the little V8 model's one-and-only race

said (and Neubauer confirmed) that he gained an important advantage by starting on the light-signal instead of the flag, which Italo Balbo, the Fascist governor of Libya, had dropped in the absent-minded manner usually adopted by civic dignitaries on such occasions.

In Italy everybody from Mussolini downwards was furious at the result, but they got little sympathy from the rest of the motor racing world, which was highly amused at the failure of their blatant attempt to exclude the Germans. It is known that one of the cars was geared to achieve 170 mph at 8000 rpm, but it is not clear which one this was. The cars were single-stage supercharged, but it is uncertain whether they had one supercharger, or two running in parallel. After the race, development work continued for some time on both the chassis and the engine. It included conversion to two-stage supercharging, as adopted for the 3-litre cars during 1939, and in this form the 1·5-litre V8's output rose to 278 bhp at 8250 rpm with 23 psi boost—a specific output of 185·95 bhp per litre.

During the war Caracciola, who had been a Swiss resident since 1929, asked if he might take over the Tripoli cars. This was agreed in principle, but foreign exchange control prevented their immediate export. Early in 1945, even before the war had ended, the two cars were actually sent by transporter to Switzerland, but Caracciola was unable to secure possession of them. After a period in the hands of the Swiss Mercedes importers the two W.165 models eventually found their way back to Stuttgart, where in 1951 a decision had already been taken to build a team of five more, to the same design, for the supercharged 1·5-litre Grand Prix formula of that time.

But the announcement of a new unsupercharged 2·5-litre formula quickly put paid to that idea. When this came into force in 1954, and Mercedes-Benz triumphantly returned to Grand Prix racing with the W.196 fuel-injection model, their new racing engine was not a V8 but a straight-eight, virtually split in two by a central power takeoff. There would not, after all, be any Phoenix-like rebirth of the little Tripoli V8.

In 1939, pondering on the way Daimler-Benz had designed and built two cars inside eight months to demonstrate their supremacy, whatever obstacles were placed in their way, the Continental correspondent of *Motor Sport* referred to their achievement as 'One of the finest things ever known in motor racing'. More than forty years later, I see no reason to disagree; it remains one of the most remarkable accomplishments in the whole history of the sport.

Chapter 3
6·3-litres

It was no easy task for a European motor manufacturer to patch up his wounds and get back into business after World War Two. For Daimler-Benz AG, it seemed almost impossible, the Board of Directors having stated flatly (but with some exaggeration) that their organization had ceased to exist in 1945. Some of the factories had been destroyed by bombing, some almost completely so, and communications had largely broken down because they were scattered between the American, French and Russian zones of occupation. Daimler-Benz therefore started in a small way in 1946 with a ten-year-old design, the model 170. It was not a time for frills or fancy specifications.

However, prosperity was recovered with amazing speed, and by 1951 Mercedes began the return to their traditional 'up-market' image with the six-cylinder ohc model 300. It had more to offer than its ultra-conservative image suggested, and the leading American magazine, *Road & Track*, went into raptures: 'Daimler-Benz AG has again produced a vehicle of remarkable character, capable of cruising long distances at high speeds with unusual passenger/driver comfort and peace of mind . . . Here is a car giving a combination of comfort, roominess and sports car handling qualities far ahead of any American sedan.' Considering the grave deficiencies of the early

double-pivot swing-axle rear suspension on the original 300, this is not so much praise for the Mercedes as a blistering condemnation of the contemporary Transatlantic blancmange.

But the 300 was to remain in production for more than twenty years, during which time it was continually updated and improved in typical Daimler-Benz fashion until barely recognizable as the same model. Half way through its production run, it had turned into an extremely well-appointed vehicle with light-alloy engine, fuel injection, a DB-designed four-speed automatic transmission, limited-slip differential, power-

The world's first petrol-injection production car was the 300 SL Gullwing coupé, announced in 1954 and destined for equal success as roadgoing product or winner of long-distance races and rallies

31

assisted steering, servo-assisted disc brakes all round, a single-pivot divided axle at the rear with an ingenious anti-dive linkage, and self-levelling pneumatic suspension. Its highly sophisticated specification and sheer build quality had, by the early Sixties, put the model 300 firmly on the leader-board with the world's best. And persistent rumour said there was something even better on the way, to give Daimler-Benz prestige an added boost. After all, the Company had dropped out of racing at the end of 1955 after accomplishing the unique feat of winning the GP Drivers' World Championship (through Juan Manuel Fangio), the European Rally Drivers' Championship (through Werner Engel), the Formula 1 Manufacturers' Championship and the Sports Car Constructors' Championship *all in the same year*. The model 300 had benefited from its obvious relationship to the 300 SL Gullwing and 300 SLR sports-racing machine, but although the smaller saloons had for some time continued to figure prominently in rallies after the withdrawal from racing, gradually they had lost ground to smaller and more nimble cars. By the early Sixties, it was indeed time for a new demonstration of Stuttgart supremacy.

This was provided in full measure when the new model 600 hit the headlines of the world's motoring Press in September 1963. From Germany, 'Unquestionably the most advanced of cars'. From America, 'The best car in the world'. From Britain, 'There is nothing in this class which offers as much'. Inevitably the model 600 was also dubbed by the Press the Grosser Mercedes, like its two pre-war predecessors, but unlike them it was available in short (10 ft 6 in) or long (12 ft 9·5 in) wheelbase, so as to offer the choice of a limousine measuring 18 ft 2 in overall, or a 'Pullman' that scaled no less than 20 ft 6 in overall. This was a splendid piece of one-

Right *Mercedes-Benz model 600: 'The best car in the world', said* Road & Track. *Even this shorter wheelbase version is more than eighteen feet long*

Above and right *First production Mercedes-Benz V8 engine, the 6·3-litre unit of the postwar Grosser or model 600, needs one-sixth of its total 300 bhp to drive the compressor for the pneumatic suspension system, the two alternators and many other auxiliaries. The eight-plunger fuel injection pump nestles out of sight between the two cylinder banks*

upmanship, for the Pullman was therefore an inch longer than the Cadillac Fleetwood 75 Imperial Limousine, and thus robbed General Motors of their *cachet* as makers of the world's biggest production car, while Rolls-Royce were left out in the cold with the modest 19 ft 10 in of their Phantom V. To a customer seeking to buy prestige for himself, these things matter. Moreover, Daimler-Benz were well aware that some heads of State would be delighted to order a 'top car' that was neither American nor British—presumably on the basis that Germany, being less Western, was therefore less decadent and less imperialist.

Except in their length and weight, the two versions of the 600 were virtually identical, the original Pullman having a longer floorpan and roof, plus an additional body-panel on each side between the front and rear doors. But even the longer 600, a four-door car like its competitors, became a sort of second-rate superlative when Mercedes offered a *six-door* Pullman body on the long wheelbase, making it a supercar of truly unrivalled visual impact. There was something about the sight of a model 600 special Pullman limousine, sitting with all six doors open, that left one lost in admiration for a manufacturer who could build nearly seven yards of automobile *and* make all those holes in the sides without having it sag in the middle.

And yet, although the sheer size of the 600 was so impressive, it had a quality of compactness,

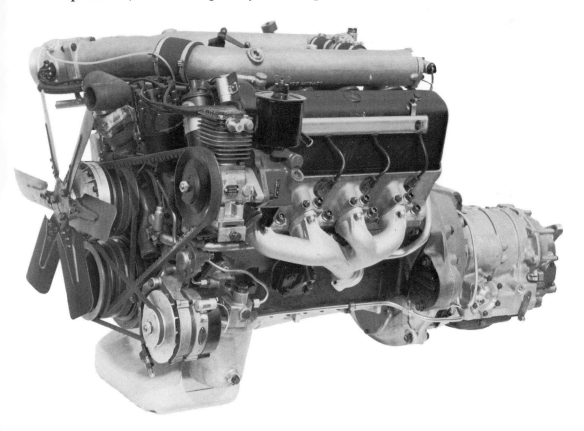

The model 600 was built on a special production line, and in 1965, its best year, output totalled 345 cars. But a decade later the oil crisis had brought the total down to a mere twenty-five cars in the year. The 600 is still available to order, but seldom built nowadays

compared to the 1938 Grosser Mercedes, that underlined the progress made in a quarter-century of automotive design. The Pullman version was exactly the same overall length as the pre-war car, but it could accommodate an additional door-opening within that length. The new car was almost a foot lower without cramping the occupants, and almost five inches narrower overall, yet the seats were substantially wider than before. With normal saloon bodywork, two out of six occupants of the 1938 Grosser were forced to sit on folding 'jump seats', but on the same wheelbase the new Pullman provided three

rows of fully-upholstered seats. It must be said,
though, that Daimler-Benz were over-hopeful in
announcing the 600 as a six-seater or eight-seater,
according to wheelbase. The US market designations, five-seater or seven-seater, were
nearer the truth.

Weight reduction was dramatic, for even in
long-wheelbase form the 600 weighed only 5820 lb
against the 8000-odd of the 1938 car. Fuel consumption was reduced by nearly fifty per cent.
The fuel-injection V8 engine of the new car
(6332 cc, though often misquoted as 6329 cc for
some reason) had a peak power output of 300 bhp
gross, compared with only 230 bhp from the pre-
war 7655 cc supercharged straight-eight. The
shorter-wheelbase version of the 600, weighing
5445 lb, was therefore able to hit 60 mph from rest
in a tyre-smoking 9·7 seconds, instead of the 17
seconds of its forebear, and the maximum speed
was increased from just over 100 mph to around
130.

The new engine, the first V8 that Daimler-Benz
had adopted for a production car, accounted for
many of these improvements. In the days of the
earlier Grosser Mercedes, a prestige car without
an imposingly long bonnet would have been a
contradiction in terms—a virility symbol without
a priapus. By the Sixties, however, it was accepted that an engine could be potent without self-
advertisement, and the 6 ft codpiece was no
longer needed. On the contrary, even a car as big
as the 600 could not spare the space required to
house a straight-eight of six or seven litres. Hence
the new V8, which was so much shorter fore-and-
aft. Apart from its cylinder layout, this first
production Mercedes V8 bore little resemblance
to their first-ever V8 unit, as used in the Tripoli
Grand Prix cars. With one chain-driven overhead
camshaft to each bank of cylinders, it was much

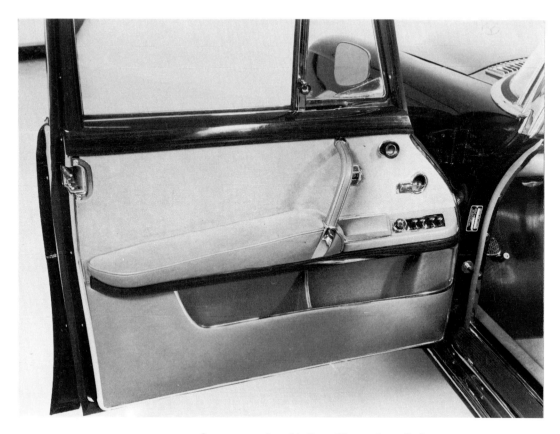

On the model 600 the windows, door locks, partition, bootlid, fuel filler flaps and front seat adjusters are all hydraulically operated

closer to the light-alloy six of the contemporary 300 SE; indeed, when Daimler-Benz were developing the V8 engine in 1959, they planned to make it of light alloy also, but decided that their casting techniques were not yet sufficiently advanced. This is intriguing to consider, bearing in mind that in 1959 Rolls-Royce announced a new 6230 cc light-alloy V8 for their Silver Cloud II and Phantom V. It may be that the requirements demanded of the Mercedes-Benz engine were more rigorous, since it had to produce about fifty per cent more power from the same capacity.

The secret of this much-enhanced power output was, of course, fuel injection. Together with the

Robert Bosch organization, Daimler-Benz had a long history of experience in this field which included extensive work on high-speed diesel engines, aircraft engines, and many experiments with their GP cars of the Thirties. The 300 SL Gullwing of 1954 was the world's first production petrol-injection car, and I remember the seemingly-unending surge of power that left me wondering if I would ever need to change gear, when I drove one at more than 150 mph on the Münich-Ingolstadt *autobahn* in 1955. The Gullwing arrangement was a six-plunger system with direct injection into the combustion chambers. For the 300 SE saloon of 1961 this was greatly simplified by using a two-plunger pump, each feeding three cylinders, with port injection. The model 600 was equipped with an eight-plunger pump but injected into the inlet ports—a compromise between the two systems which sacrificed a little of the potential high-rpm output to improve performance lower down.

The transmission system was a much-strengthened version (as it needed to be, for the 600 provided a massive 369 lb ft of torque at 2800 rpm) of the four-speed automatic with fluid coupling that Mercedes had used successfully for years, because it gave the driver much more control than torque converter systems. Using a lever marked P, R, 4, 3 and 2, the driver would normally select '4' from rest, whereupon the Grosser would start in *second* gear and make imperceptibly smooth upward changes as the road speed increased. While greater acceleration could be had by using throttle kickdown, it was smoother to override the change-points with the selector lever instead, and thus hold the intermediate ratios in engagement to higher rpm.

One-sixth of the engine's gross 300 bhp was needed to power the various automatic services:

push-button window-winding, centralized door-locking, opening and closing the boot-lid, filler flap and scuttle ventilator; adjusting the front *and* rear seats; operating the optional sun-roof and central partition. This gimmickry aroused great excitement when the 600 was announced, together with the fact that the exterior mirrors were *adjustable from inside the car*. Today, many of these features are found on quite plebeian cars, operated usually (and sometimes unreliably) by electricity. The Mercedes-Benz 600, however, reserved its electrical power for other things—such as thirteen interior lights—and its push-buttons actuated valves in a separate hydraulic power circuit, in which the pressure was maintained by an engine-driven pump. There was a compressor for the air-conditioning system, if fitted, and two three-phase alternators were driven from the engine besides the usual cooling fan, water pump and other ancillaries.

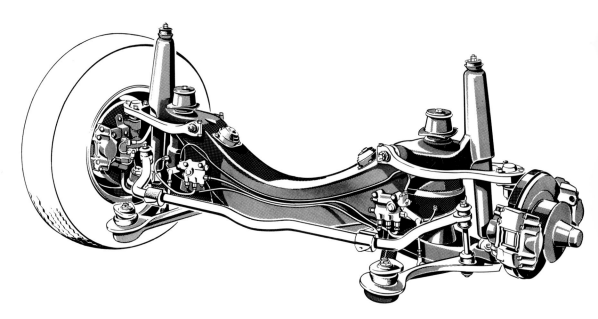

Compressed air was needed for the power-assisted steering and the highly sophisticated braking system with its dual circuit, tandem master cylinders, and two sets of calipers to each front disc.

Then there was the pressurized air suspension, for which yet another engine-driven compressor was required, with balancing valves to direct the air to each of the four 'bags' that supported the four corners of the car. Besides being self-levelling, this layout allowed the driver to increase ground clearance on thick snow or rough ground, while another control enabled him to alter the ride firmness *en route*.

There were other top cars that came closer to being a four-wheeled Hilton suite than the model 600, judged by the softness of their ride, the thickness of their carpets, the glossiness of their polished-wood fittings, or the suppleness of their seats. There were others whose engine and

Far left and below Pressurized air suspension system of the 600 is self-levelling and allows adjustment of ride firmness or ground clearance while under way. Also visible in part is the single-low-pivot layout adopted by Mercedes-Benz to reduce the ill-effects of swing-axle rear suspension

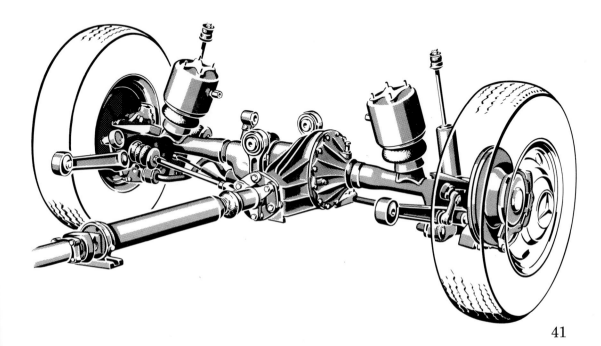

"It's for YOU!"

*"Being affluent enough to possess such
a splendid car hasn't in the least altered my attitude
to the lower orders."*

transmission were less audible when fully extended. There were others that felt substantially
bigger to drive, though in sober fact they were

The best car in the world? At 20ft 6inches overall, the model 600 Pullman is certainly the longest private car you can buy

smaller. There were a few—just a few—that would out-perform it. But there was no other car that could match the Mercedes-Benz 600 for the unique combination of comfort and performance that led Paul Frère, recognized as one of the most authoritative motoring writers, to call it simply 'The best-engineered car in the world.' To Bill Boddy of *Motor Sport* it was 'The finest luxury car I have driven ... A splendid example of Daimler-

Benz engineering at its highest pinnacle'. So utterly stable that it could be driven hands-off at 120 mph or more, the model 600 would cruise all day at this sort of speed on the *autobahn*, and its driver knew no fatigue. If other traffic encroached on the fast lane, a touch of the superb brakes would check this 2·5-ton vehicle instantly, without effort or fade, and then a firm foot on the accelerator would bring a thrust in the back as the big Mercedes returned to its usual cruising speed.

Chauffeur's delight—the long-wheelbase model 600 Pullman as seen from without and within. In typical Mercedes-Benz fashion, the facia layout is efficient and businesslike. The parking brake is applied by foot and released by hand.

45

A very rare landau version of the long-wheelbase 600, with such luxuries as a hydraulically operated hood and a TV set for rear-seat passengers. Compare this car with its pre-war equivalent, the open touring Grosser on page 19

The 600 had another, rather unexpected quality. Stanley Sedgwick, no stranger to luxury cars, said, 'The suspension was superb—especially the way in which the car could be swept through a series of fast left and right-hand bends'. *Motor Sport* noted that 'The Mercedes-Benz 600 impresses most when it is taken fast through dense traffic or hurled round corners ... It handles superbly'. *Autocar* summed it up as 'The world's biggest sports car'. And *Motor* said, 'The triumph of the Grosser Mercedes is that it combines size and complication with all the performance, safety and roadworthiness of a small car'.

It was not impossibly expensive, for it sold in Germany at little more than half its UK price (and even that much-inflated figure, it is sad to observe,

Spacious luxury of the rear compartment in a four-door Pullman, referred to by Motor as 'this mobile boardroom'

would not buy a humble 230 today). But it was undeniably thirsty, and within a decade the 1973 fuel crisis made even the wealthy aware of that fact. That year, production fell to eighty-two cars from the previous year's already low total of 210. The following year it was down to one car a week, and the British importers stopped buying for stock. By the end of 1977 they had stopped buying even to special order; a thick fog of government

regulations and restrictions barred the 600 from the USA, from Britain, and even from Continental Europe. Nowadays the Mercedes-Benz 600 survives only as the ultimate sheikmobile, built to special order for the opulent OPECs, or exchanged for a fat slice of some emergent nation's assets so that its leader may ride in style along narrow dirt roads. A car like this deserves a worthier fate.

The 6·3-litre V8 engine was also used in another memorable car which could, one day, be as sought-after by collectors as an SSKL or 540K. At the Geneva Show in March 1968, Daimler-Benz revealed that they had taken the big V8 engine of the model 600 and simply dropped it, *in toto*, into the contemporary 300SEL body shell, together with a higher final-drive ratio, better brakes and fatter tyres. It was not hard to predict the result. At Monthoux, a circuit smaller than Brands

Even the long-wheelbase Pullman, in its four-door form, seems less impressive when compared to this six-door variant of the model 600

Early in 1968, Mercedes-Benz took the 6·3-litre V8 engine of the 600 and dropped it into the 300 SEL saloon. Result: twenty-eight per cent more power for a weight increase of under 300 lb

Hatch and normally used for kart racing, Rudolf Uhlenhaut proceeded to throw this sizeable saloon around in a cloud of rubber smoke as if it were no bigger than a Mini. A few months later he repeated the performance at Laguna Seca before a

Substantially less frontal area and about 1600 lb less weight ensured high performance for the 300 SEL 6·3

delighted crowd of American journalists. Meanwhile Erich Waxenberger of the Daimler-Benz experimental division drove a similar car to victory in the Macao Six Hours, and there was speculation that the new model might serve for a triumphant return to motor racing. Indeed, in July 1969 three cars turned up to practise for the Spa 24 Hours, driven by Waxenberger, Herrmann and Ickx, but persistent tyre trouble caused their withdrawal before the start. Tests were made at several major European circuits, but plans to race the 300 SEL 6·3—if such plans existed—came to nothing in the end.

When tested, this full five-seater saloon exceeded 130 mph and accelerated from rest to 60 mph in under 7 seconds

Above *AMG of Stuttgart tried hard with this 300 SEL 6·3. Hans Heyer, here at Circuit Paul Ricard in 1971, could not turn it into a race winner however*

Top right *'Merely the greatest sedan in the world', said* Road & Track *after trying the 300 SEL 6·3*

Bottom right *Owners of ordinary 300 SEL models who failed to spot the '6·3' on the bootlid could feel quite upset when passed as if standing still by what seemed an identical car to their own*

However, the car was successfully marketed for road use, selling more than 6500 before the new S-series of late 1972 killed it off. Narrower by more than 6 inches and shorter by 21 inches than the *short* model 600, the 300 SEL 6·3 carried at least 1500 lb less weight and had a much lower frontal area. Published road-test figures vary somewhat, but the new car could reach 60 mph from rest in under 7 seconds, the exact time depending on the driver's technique to ensure that the rear tyres didn't burst into flames, and in a drag contest with a manual-shift 5·3-litre Corvette Sting Ray, the Mercedes-Benz saloon would have stayed level with the sports car all the way. Although still geared too low for top-end performance, the Mercedes would certainly exceed 130 mph, and some testers claimed about 137.

Erich Waxenberger of the Daimler-Benz experimental division drove a 300 SEL 6·3 to victory in the 1968 Macao Six Hours, and later prepared a team of three cars for the Spa 24 Hours Race. But they non-started after tyre trouble during practice

There was still ample space for five to travel in comfort, and in this respect the 300 SEL 6·3 sacrificed surprisingly little compared to the 600. The air suspension gave much the same ride, the handling was just as good, and the smaller dimensions made it even easier to throw through a succession of bends. When Paul Frère drove the car for several days, he summed it up thus: 'Among all the really top luxury cars I can think of, the Mercedes is the only one I would take out for a drive just for the fun of it, as I would do with a Ferrari, a Lamborghini or a Porsche'. *Road & Track* summed it up even more succinctly, after a full-scale road test, as 'Merely the greatest sedan in the world'.

Chapter 4
3·5-and 4·5-litres

With the model 600 judged by many to be 'the best car in the world' (except in Britain, where it was accepted in an embarrassed sort of way as *one* of the best), Daimler-Benz AG now turned to their smaller cars—several of them distinguished only by their old-fashioned looks and somewhat inadequate performance. Stuttgart would have us believe that every subsequent move was part of a master plan, but the way they juggled with bodyshells, engines, transmissions and running gear to produce a stream of 'new' models (sometimes little different from their predecessors, and with a lifespan of mayfly-like brevity) seems oddly haphazard in retrospect. Trying hard to see the entire wood as well as all the trees, I think the policy of 'co-ordinated integration' was indeed being followed, but at first it wasn't co-ordinated enough. They were certainly 'getting it together' rather slowly. Sometimes a new engine or suspension system would be ready for production some years before the bodyshell it was intended for, or vice versa, and it seemed that Mercedes would rather use the unit to modify an existing model—even for a year or two—than leave it to gather dust on the factory floor.

This was all very well, but the original type designations soon lost all meaning, and instead of adopting a new system that made sense, Daimler-Benz clung stubbornly to the old one, causing

First quantity-production V8 engine made by Mercedes was the 3·5-litre cast-iron unit which came out in September 1969. In European tune, it gave 200 bhp

everlasting confusion to the public, their own dealers, motoring historians and (as I was to discover) to the Company executives also. A man who embarks, for example, on a detailed list of all mutants in the 250/280 range, home and overseas, will realize sadly that that way madness lies.

So the story of the 3·5-litre and 4·5-litre V8 Mercedes-Benz saloons is a tortuous one, partly because the logic (if any) is obscure, and partly because other body styles keep getting in on the act. The 3·5-litre engine was first presented in a rather old-fashioned convertible, an equally dated coupé and a scarcely-new saloon. After nearly two years it turned up again in two other saloons, also quite long-established, and soon afterwards the first two 3·5-litres were replaced by completely new models in the SL/SLC category. Another delay, then the engine was fitted in a completely new saloon belonging to the so-called New S Class. Eventually this was supplemented by a longer-wheelbase version of the same car, but meanwhile the 3·5-litre engine had been enlarged

to 4·5 litres for the American market, where it was
sold either exclusively or optionally in various
models, both old and new. In 1973 the larger
engine came onto the world market to power four
new cars, open and closed, but in late 1979 it was
revealed that yet another new range—*also* called
the New S Class, presumably to distinguish it
from the New S Class of late 1972—had been
developed. At the time of writing, eight of the 3·5-
lire and 4·5-litre models are still in production,
but some are being phased out to make room for
their successors; others will continue to be built
for the US market. During the production life of
all these V8 models several highly significant
changes in specification have been made, not all
of them clearly recorded outside (or even inside)
the factory.

Perhaps it is reasonable to start in January
1968 with the New Generation, which was not a
pop-music group but a range of new or revised
models, six of which (known within the factory as
Series 114/115) had a new small bodyshell with
anti-dive front suspension, and what Daimler-
Benz called *Diagonal-Pendelachse* at the rear.
Literally this means 'diagonal swing-axle', but
actually it was a semi-trailing-arm layout not
unlike BMW's system. At last Stuttgart had
started moving away from their much-loved swing
axles, either in double-pivot form or the highly
effective, but unduly complicated, single-pivot
arrangement they had developed to minimize
final-oversteer effects. Yet the unfortunate model
300 was stuck with its existing (Series 109)
bodyshell, it missed out on the new suspension,
and it lost the light-alloy 2996 cc six-cylinder
engine inherited from the Gullwing 300 SL. Instead, it was given a cast-iron 2778 cc six which
provided less torque and had to rev higher for the
same power output. This hard-pressed unit

seemed a far cry from the glamorous 6·3-litre V8 of the model 600, and when the 6·3 was made available in the 300 SEL bodyshell soon after, it merely emphasized the yawning gap that existed in the Mercedes-Benz engine range.

That gap remained unfilled for nearly two years, until the new 3·5-litre V8 engine came out at the Frankfurt Show in September 1969. This was an excellent modern unit, borrowing not one major component from earlier engines but making good use of their best design features. It had a cast-iron block carried down below the line of the crankshaft, which was predictably short but fully counterbalanced and carried in five stout main bearings. The cylinder heads (which were interchangeable) and sump were cast in aluminium. To each cylinder bank there was an overhead camshaft, chaindriven, with rocking fingers between cams and valve-stems. Everything about the engine spelt designed-in strength (the safe rpm limit was quoted as 6500), and the dimensions were so massively oversquare, with 92 mm bore and 65·8 mm stroke, that everyone guessed the capacity of 3499 cc would later be increased by substituting a longer-throw crankshaft. The automatic transmission made available for the new engine followed customary Daimler-Benz practice, being a four-speeder with fluid coupling.

In European form the new V8 gave 200 bhp at 5800 rpm, and the maximum torque was improved to 211 lb ft, but at the fairly high engine speed of 4000 rpm. There was transistorized ignition—seldom seen outside the race-tracks in those days—and an electronic fuel-injection system which was in fact the D-Jetronic developed by Bosch for Volkswagen, from a design pioneered by Bendix in America. Arranged to cut off fuel delivery on over-run, this and the new ignition system helped to reduce exhaust pollution. For

The oldish 300 SEL with its Series 109 bodyshell and old-type suspension was the first Mercedes saloon to be fitted with the new 3·5-litre V8 engine. It was called the 300 SEL 3·5

U 78851

Above and right In February 1971 the new 3·5-litre engine was also made available in the 280 SE (Series 108) bodyshell, still with the older single-pivot swing-axle rear suspension. This made it a 125 mph saloon, so it also had fatter tyres and ventilated disc brakes

America, however, it was also necessary to weaken the mixture and retard the ignition so much that at one part of the curve it was 16° behind the optimum setting.

At its debut the new engine was installed in two rather old Series 111 body types, the 280 SE fixed-head coupé and convertible, plus the 300 SEL saloon. Naturally these cars performed much better (except in the USA) than they had done as 2·8-litres, and the saloon sold well. The others were less successful, although they at least looked different, having been given a lower and wider front grille to suit the compact V8 engine.

In February 1971 the 3·5-litre engine was put into the 280 SE and 280 SEL saloons (Series 108) for the world market. Britain opted out of the longer-wheelbase saloon, and asked for a special 'package' on the 280 SE (including twin vertical headlamps) to distinguish it from its six-cylinder ancestor. Not everyone would spot that the 280 SE 3·5 had ventilated-disc brakes and fatter tyres in deference to its 125 mph maximum and acceleration to match. America decided to have neither of these saloons in 3·5-litre form, and elsewhere the 280 SEL 3·5 was outsold 10 to 1 by the 300 SEL 3·5.

Three months later, Daimler-Benz invited the Press to see a new V8-powered two-seater convertible (or roadster) known as the 350 SL, followed at the end of the year by a lengthened version with fixed steel top, the 350 SLC coupé. Although the internal code (Series 107) suggests a long development period, these were the first cars marketed with the new engine allied to the new suspension system that had previously been seen only on the Series 114/115 saloons of January 1968. *Road & Track* exulted in 'sophisticated

The 280 SEL, like the shorter-wheelbase 280 SE, could also be bought with the 3·5-litre V8 engine, but not in Britain. America imported neither of these cars with the 3·5-litre engine installed

suspension geometry that . . . allows a slight, easily controllable oversteer to be induced by a burst of power or a quickly lifted throttle foot—a delight to the experienced driver but no threat to the inexperienced'. Yet they were heavy cars compared to the earlier 280 SL, having steel panels instead of aluminium to meet American crash-resistance regulations, so the acceleration was leisurely even without emission-control gear. With it, the 350 SL and SLC would have been sluggish indeed.

So the factory, as expected, lengthened the piston stroke to 85 mm and turned the 3·5-litre into a high-torque 4·5-litre. For this larger engine they also produced a new three-speed automatic transmission with torque converter. When the 350 SL was first exported to the USA in the summer of 1971, it was therefore supplied as the '350 SL 4·5', with 4·5-litre engine and three-speed automatic transmission; there was, indeed, no manual gearbox that could have taken the torque. The 3·5-litre 280 SE coupé and convertible were quietly dropped after less than two years' production, the 4·5-litre engine was made optionally available to American buyers of the 280 SE saloon, and it was standardized in US-specification 280 SEL and 300 SEL saloons. As the engine did not officially exist at that time, Stuttgart took care to conceal it from customers elsewhere. If an American took delivery of his 350 SEL 4·5 or similar model in Europe, it was handed over with a '3·5' badge on the back, and he had to get the car to the far side of the Atlantic before being given a '4·5' badge to replace it.

Long before the 4·5-litre V8 engine was announced in Europe, it was standardized for US-specification 280 SEL sedans. This car, though now UK-registered, was originally sold in America, as revealed by its twin vertical headlamps and 'running lights', then required by Federal regulations

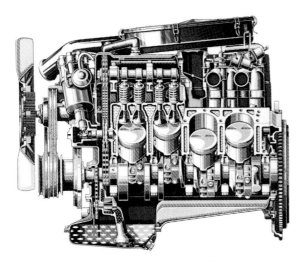 

With a piston stroke of only 65·8 mm to its 92 mm bore, the 3·5-litre V8 was massively oversquare. It was not hard to predict that Mercedes would later lengthen the stroke to increase the capacity, as they did when turning it into the 4·5-litre version

However, coupé and convertible models are really the preserve of L. J. K. Setright, who covered this subject with his customary expertise in *Mercedes-Benz Roadsters*, an earlier title in the AutoHistory series. We still had to wait quite some time for the V8 engine to be offered in a new saloon bodyshell with up-to-date suspension. It came in September 1972, when the first of the New S Class appeared at the Paris Salon. The new Series 116 bodyshell was available as a 280 S or 280 SE saloon with dohc six-cylinder engine, or as a new 3·5-litre V8-powered saloon, the 350 SE, which was to replace the 3·5-litre versions of the 280 SE/SEL and the old but highly-respected 300 SEL saloons. None of these was sold in the USA, for there were others to come that would suit that market better. Later, too, came a long-wheelbase 350 SEL saloon, which Britain declined; after all, the 'short' 350 SE was already longer in the wheelbase than the 'long' 300 SEL.

Undoubtedly handsome, the new Series 116 bodyshell followed the seemingly inevitable trend imposed by government regulations, for it was longer, wider and heavier than before without

*One of Daimler-Benz AG
Bildarchiv's own publicity
photographs of 1964 – the
'standard' 600 with whitewall
tyres*

Far Left *A slightly later Model 600 shot in California's sunshine. Note the Federal headlamps*

Above *Another North American specification V8 – this time it's an early 4.5-litre 300SEL photographed in England*

Left *Daimler-Benz show off contemporary German fashion in both clothes and cars – home market version of the 280SE 3.5*

Far Left *DB have long persisted in using painted road wheel hub caps as on this 350SE. Metallic paint is an oft used option too*

Left *Defining the model is a problem. This high speed shot captures a 450SE*

Below *A beautiful car before a part of a beautiful country house in the English landscape – UK version of the 450SEL 6.9 with option alloy wheels*

Left *1979 Mercedes-Benz*
450SEL

Above *Not quite the most*
costly, that's the SEL – here's
the 500SE

Top *Latest V8 offering from*
DB – 380SE in home market
trim

The new New S Class. For comparison the 280 6 cylinder version sits on the left while the 380 and then the 500SEs reveal all on the right

offering additional passenger space. This meant, alas, that the 3·5-litre V8 engine provided less performance in the New S Class body than it had done in the older bodyshells, the 350 SE taking 1·5 seconds longer to reach 60 mph and having a top speed about 3 mph lower. Even a 200 bhp engine may be disappointing in a car that weighs something over 3700 lb, and the shortage of bottom-end torque was no help. To some extent this was compensated for by the new three-speed automatic transmission which had been developed for the 4·5-litre engine. It had also been fitted from August 1972 onwards to the 3·5-litre 350 SL/SLC, and it now became the standard option for the 350 SE from its inception. According to *Motor*, 'The new transmission is one of the best automatics we have tried. Apart from a slight change in engine note, it's very difficult to detect when the gearchanges occur', Which was just as well, for if you wanted to drive a 350 SE fast in

Alongside the dohc six-cylinder engine, the V8 reveals the compact dimensions achieved with this cylinder configuration

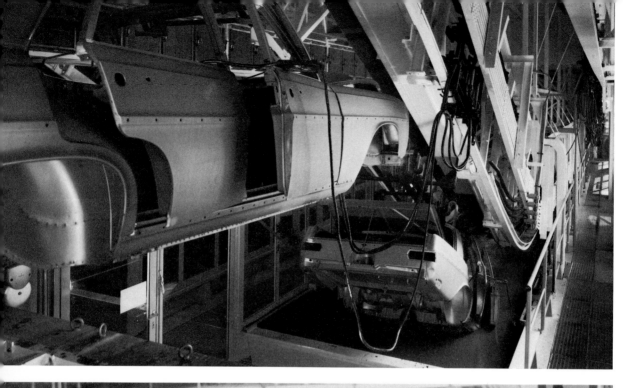

Britain, gearchanges (whether by kickdown or over-ride) had to occur pretty frequently.

The saving grace of the New S Class was its suspension system, as Daimler-Benz belong to the élite band of manufacturers who rank active safety equally with passive, whatever Ralph Nader may dredge up from his profound ignorance of automotive engineering. The controlled-crush bodywork was accompanied by a superb design which added greatly to the high-speed stability of a model range that already excelled in this respect. The semi-trailing-arm rear suspension was that introduced with the Series 114/115 saloons and further developed in the 350 SL/SLC roadster and coupé, but the front suspension derived from Stuttgart's remarkable Wankel-engined C.111 experimental car, a mid-engined mobile testbed that had been 'designed from the driver's seat outwards'. Its zero-offset geometry and progressive anti-dive characteristics brought new standards to the world of the stockbroker's

Far left The new Series 116 bodyshell (here in the top picture going through paint dip) was at last announced in September 1972 as the New S Class. The lower factory picture shows how the cars are placed on runners, so that the wheels remain stationary while they are pushed along the assembly line on built-in rollers

Below left and right With the advent of the Series 116, the V8 engine was mated to the magnificent new suspension system whose features included a zero-offset layout at the front end and a semi-trailing-arm arrangement at the rear. This was a major step forward

limousine, and as *Motor* commented, 'There are few sports cars, let alone large saloons, that could keep up with a well-driven 350SE on a winding road'.

At the Geneva Show of March 1973, Mercedes-Benz finally admitted to the existence of the 4·5-litre V8 engine—two years after it had first been supplied to American buyers! The new 450SL roadster, 450SLC coupé and 450SE saloon were of course developments of their 3·5-litre counterparts, but the 450SEL long-wheelbase saloon actually preceded the 350SEL, being prompted by complaints of limited legroom in the back of the 350SE (despite its being longer than the old 300SEL). All four of the new cars were to be sold in the UK and the USA. All four were fitted 'as standard' with the three-speed torque converter transmission that had recently become available for the 3·5-litre cars, but when used with the 4·5-litre engine it was of a tougher design. And it

Purposeful front view of the 350SE is in sharp contrast to the 'early perpendicular' lines of the 300SEL and its contemporaries. The wiper pivots are surprisingly close together, and by the standards of 1972 the rear-view mirror is enormous

needed to be, for torque was the outstanding quality of the bigger V8 engine in European tune. Power output was increased only modestly, to 225 bhp at 5000 rpm, although this was a very desirable 800 rpm lower down the scale than the 3·5-litre's peak output. The maximum torque, however, went from 211 lb ft at 4000 rpm to a solid 278 at only 3000, and the curve was so flat that the 4·5 could produce more torque at little more than tickover (217 lb ft at 1000 rpm) than the 3·5 could at four times the engine speed. In fully detoxed

German law requires that the ringed Mercedes star mascot must be pivoted to minimize accidental injuries. Which tells us that this high-speed shot of a 350 SE is no fake—when the badge is bending backwards like this, the car is really covering the ground

Above *Although the 4·5-litre V8 engine had powered US-specification cars since mid-1971, not until 1973 did the factory admit to its existence in Europe by unveiling the 450 SE saloon*

Right *The Mercedes-Benz W3A 040 transmission system, a new three-speed type with torque converter, was mated to the 4·5-litre V8 engine for use in cars supplied to the USA. Later this same transmission was supplied with 3·5-litre cars in Europe, but for European 4·5-litre models Daimler-Benz developed a tougher version known as the W3B 050*

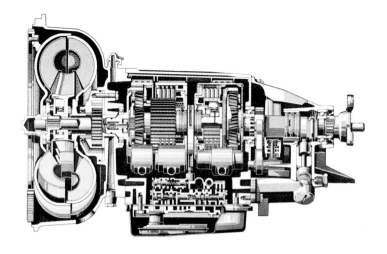

form, unfortunately, the bigger engine's extra litre only just compensated for the stifling effect of emission-control equipment.

Nor was this much-improved engine the whole story. As another example of their very positive approach to road safety, Stuttgart now incorporated in the S Class suspension a new device called a 'starting torque compensator'. This was an anti-squat linkage on the rear axle which not only discouraged a nose-up, tail-down attitude under hard initial acceleration, but also contributed to anti-dive control under heavy braking. *Motor Sport* observed, 'It only requires a test run in any of the 450 S series to realize how incredibly effective it is. Under the harshest acceleration, even with a load on board, the tail refuses to dip to upset passenger comfort. What is even more impressive is the almost uncanny effect this system (which also keeps rear wheel camber constant) has on braking. Its effect is to pull the tail down slightly . . . When the servo-assisted, dual-circuit disc brakes are applied the car feels to glue itself down to the tarmac'.

So far as performance was concerned, *Motor* conceded that the bigger engine more than restored what had earlier been lost with the adoption of the heavier Series 116 bodyshell. While admitting that the steering, ride, handling and brakes were definitely better than before, they thought it 'a pity this excellent ride is marred by relatively poor suppression of road noise'. With what seemed like an air of faint disapproval, they reported that one of their testers had called the 450 SEL the best car he'd ever driven. Eight months earlier, it is interesting to note, *Road & Track* had said, 'The Mercedes characteristics will not appeal to everyone. . . . If you enjoy involvement with your driving and are interested in knowing what the wheels are doing at any

At the end of 1973, a panel of motoring journalists voted the new Mercedes-Benz 450 SE as 'Car of the Year' in recognition of its many outstanding qualities. Said the committee's chairman, Paul Frère, 'It was time Daimler-Benz got acknowledgement for cars of an overall quality and technical merit second to none'

instant and why, then the 450 is your kind of car. . . . The stability and feeling of security conveyed to the driver, whether driving in a straight line or cornering, are extremely high. . . . The 450 takes smooth and rough roads with equal aplomb even when driven hard. As a roadgoing sedan it has no equal'.

The problem was, of course, to find some generally-accepted basis for comparison. A steady hardening of the Deutschemark had made the 450 SE/SEL a very expensive car in both the UK and the USA, although Mercedes prices varied considerably from country to country (as they do today) because of different profit margins, different import duties, and the list of 'options' included in an importer's standard specification. In Britain, the Mercedes was usually compared unfavourably with the Jaguar XJ12, which cost half as much and provided rather better performance. The Americans, however, could buy a 450 SEL saloon for only forty per cent more than the Jaguar, and in any case seemed to reject the notion that quality could be measured with a stopwatch. *Road & Track* wound up their test report by saying, 'Mercedes cars are not built to a price, but to the highest attainable level of excellence.... The 450 owner won't mind having spent a bundle more—he knows he's bought the best'.

And at the end of 1973 a panel of forty-five motoring journalists in Europe chose the Mercedes-Benz 450 series as the Car of the Year. Soon after, *Motor* remarked primly that 'The 450 can only be regarded by many as over-large, ostentatious and wasteful of fuel' (though in fact it used less than the XJ12). A little later Paul Frère, chairman of the European Car of the Year committee, put his own views on record: 'Though the big Mercedes-Benz is surely not very compatible with the current fuel shortage and speed limits from which most of Europe suffers, I personally feel that a car designed in and for happier days must not be judged in the context of the current misery. Also, it was high time Daimler-Benz got acknowledgement for producing cars of an overall quality and technical merit that is certainly second to none. They may be expensive, but they are worth every penny you pay for them if you can afford to. Just remember, a 450 SE costs about half as much as a Rolls-Royce Silver Shadow.'

The 3·5-litre cars continued in production side-by-side with the bigger V8s, so that by late 1975 the Mercedes-Benz range included no less than eleven V8-engined models: the original 6·3-litre model 600, still built to special order in two different wheelbases; the 350/450 SL roadsters with folding soft-top and detachable steel top; the

350/450 SLC two-door fixed-head coupés; the
350/450 SE saloons; their longer-wheelbase
350/450 SEL counterparts, and the new high-
performance car that forms the subject of the next
chapter.

In October 1975 the 4·5-litre engines, and in
January 1976 the 3·5-litres, were modified in two
significant respects. Although an electronically-
actuated intermittent injection system seemed
ideal by comparison with the earlier Diesel-style
mechanically-driven types, there were certain
disadvantages in the pressure-measuring (*Druck-
messung*) principle of the D-Jetronic, which was
not only expensive to make but also rather
inflexible in its applications. It was therefore
replaced by the mechanically-controlled
continuous-injection K-Jetronic (*Kontinuier-
liche*) system, which was not only simpler but also
more adaptable to future requirements in exhaust
emission control. At the same time, the fulcrum
points of the steel 'fingers' interposed between
camshaft and valve-stem were fed with engine oil
under pressure, making them function in the same
way as hydraulic tappets (but more efficiently so)
to quieten the valvegear and eliminate any need
for periodic adjustment.

Twenty-five years ago, a colleague and I travelled from Munich to Frankfurt in a 300 SL Gullwing, cruising at 120 mph so far as heavy *autobahn*
traffic allowed, and we averaged just over 78 mph
on this 250-mile trip, which I remember as hot,
noisy and uncomfortable. A few months ago, I
travelled over 100-odd miles of the same route for
the same reason—to catch a plane whose depar-
ture time seemed uncomfortably close—but on
this occasion we were three-up in a 450 SE saloon.
Again we cruised at 120 mph when possible, but
the traffic was heavier and we averaged little
more than 80 mph. The big Mercedes wafted us

The 4·5-litre saloon is here seen in its long-wheelbase form as the 450 SEL, a car offering exceptional comfort and performance for autobahn *use, but now being phased out in favour of the most recent 380 and 500 models announced late in 1979*

along in near-soundless comfort, except that the fresh-air ventilation system began to howl at anything much over 130. Not enough to disturb our companion in the back, however; he slept for the entire journey.

In late 1975 the 4·5-litre V8 engines, and in early 1976 the 3·5-litres, switched from D-Jetronic (Below right) to K-Jetronic fuel injection (Below left)

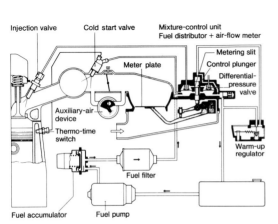

Injection valve
Cold start valve
Mixture-control unit
Fuel distributor + air-flow meter
Metering slit
Meter plate
Control plunger
Differential-pressure valve
Auxiliary-air device
Thermo-time switch
Warm-up regulator
Fuel filter
Fuel accumulator
Fuel pump

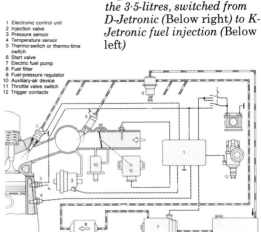

1 Electronic control unit
2 Injection valve
3 Pressure sensor
4 Temperature sensor
5 Thermo-switch or thermo-time switch
6 Start valve
7 Electric fuel pump
8 Fuel filter
9 Fuel-pressure regulator
10 Auxiliary-air device
11 Throttle valve switch
12 Trigger contacts

Chapter 5
6·9-litres

A sad side-effect of the New S Class's arrival in 1972 was that it killed off the 300 SEL bodyshell, and with it Europe's favourite motorway cruiser, the 300 SEL 6·3. At the time it was still selling steadily, and some owners were anxious to buy another, the earliest examples being then three years old. Daimler-Benz assured them a replacement was on the way. Neither they nor anyone else knew that this 135 mph limousine would have no successor for a further three years, at least.

The formula seems simple enough: take the best bodyshell in your current range, cram the largest available engine into it, and there you are. However, Stuttgart's methods were no longer as crudely direct as that. In this case they were very keen to refine the basic concept a great deal, and some of those refinements had to keep step with developments elsewhere in the model range. Then there was the fuel crisis of late 1973, making it a tactless time to announce a large car with the kind of performance that causes any self-respecting conservationist to go purple with righteous indignation. So although the new 450 SEL 6·9 Mercedes-Benz could have been released at the 1974 Geneva Show, if not sooner, they decided to hold it back for another year. Even then, it was to be a low-profile exercise because there was a waiting-list of several hundred who wanted the car *now*, whatever its

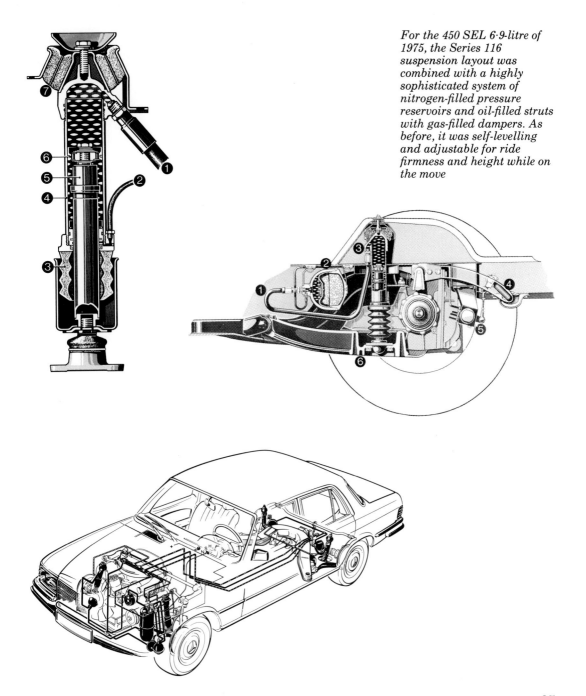

For the 450 SEL 6·9-litre of 1975, the Series 116 suspension layout was combined with a highly sophisticated system of nitrogen-filled pressure reservoirs and oil-filled struts with gas-filled dampers. As before, it was self-levelling and adjustable for ride firmness and height while on the move

Based on the 6·3-litre engine of the Grosser Mercedes, the new 6·9-litre V8 gave fifteen per cent more power, and Stuttgart's many detail improvements made the unit maintenance-free for its first 50,000 miles

specification might be. Shown to the European press in May 1975, the new model was still unobtainable in Britain or America until late 1976.

The engine was of course the 6·3-litre V8, but modified and developed until little other than the 95 mm piston stroke remained. Bored out to 107 mm, it became even more oversquare than before and the capacity was increased to 6834 cc. It had the K-Jetronic injection and ingenious hydraulic-fulcrum rocker arms that were also being adopted for the smaller-capacity V8 engines, plus fully transistorized contactless ignition and a new type of head gasket by Reinz-Repa (generally but incorrectly called Ferrolastic) which made periodic tightening-down

Extensive testing and development work ensured unrivalled stability at high speed in the new 450 SEL 6·9-litre, which was arguably the world's finest motorway cruiser

unnecessary. A change to dry-sump lubrication made it easier to fit the engine into the Series 116 bodyshell, and almost doubled the total oil capacity. With these modifications, said Daimler-Benz, the engine could be virtually left to its own devices for the first 50,000 miles of its life. Maximum power output was 286 bhp at 4250 rpm, and maximum torque 405 lb ft at 3000 rpm, representing improvements of almost 15 and 10 per cent respectively over the 6·3-litre engine's performance, and at just a few hundred rpm more.

But high performance, Professor Dr Hans Scherenberg insisted, was merely a by-product of the Company's search for greater all-round driving comfort. The increased engine output was partly to compensate for increased weight, and part of that was accounted for by something special. Far out of sight under the now-familiar 450 SEL bodyshell was a new suspension system that Daimler-Benz referred to as 'hydro-pneumatic', though some such term as 'oleo-gas'

The 260 km/h (162 mph) speedometer of the 450 SEL 6·9 did not flatter too wildly. Although only 140 mph was claimed by Mercedes, Motor *saw a two-way mean 144, and Paul Frère drove another example at 148 mph. For a full-sized luxury saloon, that's quick*

might have been nearer the mark. Like most things emanating from Stuttgart, it was the result of continual development work—and although nobody cared to mention the fact, it also solved a serious problem. The self-levelling air suspension eventually standardized on the 300 SEL had had a distressing habit of giving way somewhere, when the car was stationary, if the balancing valves became faulty. The car would cheerfully sit up again as soon as the engine started, of course, but no Mercedes owner enjoyed finding his pride and joy collapsed in a corner like a sick camel. The S Class cars had reverted to steel springs for the semi-trailing-arm suspension of Series 116 models, with (later on) the option of an engine-driven self-levelling device at the rear.

More costly than the ordinary 450 SEL by more than £11,000, the 6·9-litre could only be recognized by its fatter tyres and '6·9' badge on the boot-lid. The very rich and modest could even have the badge omitted

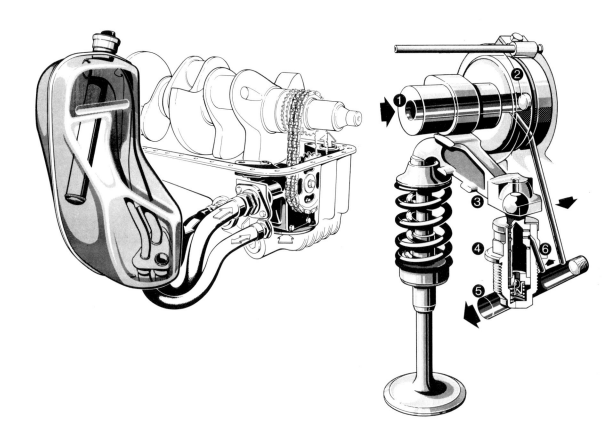

Dry-sump lubrication reduced engine height to get the 6·9-litre tucked under the 450 SEL bonnet, and new refinements included an ingenious hydraulic-fulcrum rocker arm, later adopted for the smaller V8 engines and still used on the latest 3·8 and 5·0-litre models

This was now further developed for the 6·9-litre version of the 450 SEL by eliminating the steel springs again, front and rear, and combining the otherwise standard Series 116 suspension with a highly sophisticated arrangement of nitrogen-filled pressure reservoirs and oil-filled struts, the latter incorporating gas-filled dampers. It was self-levelling, it provided full spring travel at all times, and the ride height could be adjusted on the move, either to compensate for a heavy load on board or to increase the ground clearance when required. The effect was to combine all the tautness and stability of S Class suspension (including its anti-dive and anti-squat controls) with the additional comfort of fluid suspension, while eliminating the pitch and wallow of Citroën's somewhat similar system.

Daimler-Benz claimed a maximum of 140 mph for the new saloon (though some testers put it much closer to 150) with 0–60 mph acceleration in under 7·4 seconds. To put it another way, this meant they had produced a four-seater luxury limousine with the performance of the contemporary Maserati Khamsin or V12 Jaguar E type. At the time of the press preview, the tax-paid German price was said to be about DM65,000, then the equivalent of $28,000 or £12,000. The ordinary 450SEL was then selling for almost £11,000 in Britain, and the cheapest Rolls-Royce cost nearly £15,000. However, when the 450SEL 6·9 eventually reached the UK in late 1976, the price had somehow climbed to £22,000, and Rolls-Royce were selling their Silver Shadow II at £22,800. In early 1979 the gap was even wider— £28,600 for the Mercedes and £32,000 for the Rolls—but by the end of the same year the German car had a £30,500 price tag to a staggering £36,650 for the British one. The two were no longer even in the same price-bracket.

At first acquaintance with the car, *Autocar* said, 'The quality of the Stuttgart development engineers, all keen drivers and with the authority to back it up, shows through at every corner. . . . It is only the driver who can appreciate why this car costs so much'. *Road & Track*, though based less than forty miles from Hollywood, ran right out of new superlatives and called it 'The fastest, best sedan in the world'. A little later, *Motor* (who had been very lukewarm

91

A 450 SEL 6·9 is pictured at Nice, where the first Mercedes cars showed their paces eighty years ago, Werner winning the Nice race by half-an-hour on 25 March 1901 and La Turbie hillclimb four days later

about the ordinary 450 SEL a couple of years earlier) went wild about the 6·9-litre after a fuller test: 'Exclusive, fast, immensely safe and beautifully made. . . . Without doubt the greatest Mercedes yet. . . . A first-class showcase of outstanding technological achievements'. But *Autocar*, later still, swung the opposite way to compare the Mercedes unfavourably with the cheaper (in

England) Aston Martin V8 and the very much cheaper Jaguar XJ 5·3. They omitted to mention that the Silver Shadow II (then costing £3400 more than the Mercedes) took nearly twice as long to achieve three figures, had a top speed at least 25 mph lower, used appreciably more petrol and was arguably less comfortable than its German equivalent.

Some people find it difficult, even impossible, to understand the appeal of the 450 SEL 6·9. Here was a car that looked *exactly* the same as another Mercedes costing £11,000 *less* in Britain at the time of writing. Only the fatter tyres and a little '6·9' badge on the tail gave the game away (and you could, if you wished, have the badge left off). On the road, this superlative vehicle could even be mistaken for one of the still smaller models at perhaps a third of its price. It was therefore poles apart from the Wagnerian splendour of the model 600 Pullman, or the flamboyance of the pre-war Grosser Mercedes. In terms of subtlety, you might as well compare a performance by Sir Alec Guinness with a turn by Danny La Rue.

It follows, then, that if one's car is intended primarily to be a status symbol proclaiming one's opulence to all, this last of the big-engined Mercedes-Benz was much too unobtrusive to serve. For that, the popular choice runs to a taller radiator shell surmounted by a different mascot. Cars are, like clothes, a matter of personal taste, and not everybody who can afford a Pucci shirt will wear it with the label hanging out. Some enjoy the blatant swagger of a blood-red supercar that makes every head turn—including, alas, those in peaked uniform caps with a checkered band around them. Others prefer something very unpretentious-looking, in which it is possible to travel at a consistently higher speed without attracting any attention whatsoever.

The 6·9-litre Mercedes was built in a country without overall speed limits, where cars are still driven fast over considerable distances, and designed by men who know exactly what a driver needs in order to motor safely and fast for long periods at a stretch, solo or in company, with absolute confidence and comfort. Besides the usual conveniences of a luxury saloon—electric window-lifts, centralized door-locking, air conditioning, headlamp wash/wipe, etc—there are less obvious features like ingeniously ribbed rear lights that remain clean in wet weather, heat-absorbing glass all round, a laminated windscreen *and* rear window, head-rests and safety belts for all passengers, automatic transmission with cruise control, and a ZF limited-slip differential.

The seats are quite firm—too firm, some testers insisted—but a long journey proves they offer support in the right places. The steering wheel is slightly larger than modern fashion dictates, because Daimler-Benz have studied this, as they have studied everything else, and believe that a large wheel encourages a more relaxed, less aggressive style of driving. The instruments, too, sacrifice nothing to the whimsies of some styling department: a large, circular 160 mph speedometer dead in front of the driver is flanked by a tachometer (redlined at 5250 rpm) and a cluster of fuel gauge, oil pressure gauge and coolant thermometer. Like all the controls, the gear selector is perfectly placed and works with a precision that is sheer joy.

Forward visibility is excellent, and as usual the big three-pointed star serves as a convenient sight for aiming this projectile. As one accelerates to a three-figure cruising speed (in twenty seconds or less) one can not only feel oneself being thrust back into the seat, but also hear a subdued snarl from the engine and transmission. If this annoys you, the Mercedes is not your sort of car—but how can it be irritating to hear beautifully assembled machinery doing its job so willingly? And telling you somehow that you may rely on it to continue doing so indefinitely, for the message it conveys is that Daimler-Benz inspectors disapprove of *Freitag* cars.

Again, although the suspension system is one of the most sophisticated ever designed, it will give audible warning of a major change in road surface, and this may either please or infuriate you, depending on the amount of cotton wool you want to have around you in a fast car. This is one of the roomiest cars there is, having more legroom and interior width than a Rolls or a Cadillac, yet it can be chucked about like a good sports car—which means it can be parked or manœuvered in heavy traffic with equal ease. With probably the best power-assisted steering and brakes in the world, it is totally under the driver's control at all times, and does without effort exactly what it is told to do. To these virtues, one other must be added. Besides being amazingly stable at high speed, either when cornering or when running straight, the 6·9-litre also *feels* stable, which is not the same thing at all. Some people place more value on this than others do, and I am emphatically one of them.

At one time, Stuttgart planned to update the model 600 to bring it more in line with 450 SEL 6·9 specification, but it would have involved more work than Grosser sales justified. So the 6·3-litre model 600, which is still available (at a price), is in many ways an old-fashioned car compared to the 6·9-litre, which has now reached the end of its production life. In years to come we may look back on the 6·9 as being—within its own genre—the ultimate expression of automotive design.

Chapter 6
3·8~and 5·0~litres

Professor Werner Breitschwerdt, head of development at Daimler-Benz, bases the latest S Class designs on the belief that even in an oil-starved world, people will continue to want cars they can drive fast and safely

Seven years after the New S Class (Series 116) had been announced, the 1979 Frankfurt Show marked the launching of its successor, the new New S Class (Series 126), with a completely redesigned body and a range of three engines: the six-cylinder 2·8-litre in somewhat improved form, and two light-alloy V8s, one of 3·8 and the other of 5·0 litres. A month later, together with four other British journalists, I attended a press conference near Stuttgart, where we were invited to drive the new cars and talk to Daimler-Benz's development experts about the thinking that lay behind their introduction.

It was, after all, a time when concern over the energy crisis had approached hysteria level in some quarters, and only the makers of mouse-powered matchboxes on wheels could hope to escape stern criticism from the more earnest citizens. However, Professor Werner Breitschwerdt, head of the development department, told us quite clearly that Mercedes had decided to do things *their* way. 'The average annual mileage for S Class cars is 16,000, which means they cover about twice as many miles as the statistical average of all cars. The percentage distance driven in towns, in this class of vehicle, is appreciably lower than average; the motorway mileage is very much higher. Our S Class cars, which are the workplace of so many, must have an adequate amount of room combined with a high degree of safety. People expect to be able to drive in them over long distances in a relaxed manner, safely and without getting fatigued. . . . Our view [is] that cars of the size of our S Class will continue to be needed in twenty or thirty years' time. . . . We believe that top speed, acceleration and vehicle size must be maintained'.

Stuttgart therefore rejected the idea of merely sizing-down the 3·5- and 4·5-litre models, with the loss of performance and comfort that such a policy would almost certainly have brought in its wake. Instead, they concentrated on two things: a very subtle reshaping of the bodyshell to minimize aerodynamic drag, and the greatest possible weight reduction overall without losing structural rigidity. The result of the first exercise was startling, for although the car's appearance was altered very little, Daimler-Benz claimed a fourteen per cent improvement, quoting a drag coefficient of only 0·36—which caused a few eyebrows to be raised disbelievingly in the motor

The subtle differences between New S Class (Series 116) and the new New S Class (Series 126) can be seen by comparing this 500 SE with the 350 SE on page 77

Four examples of what Daimler-Benz call their S Class models (though it is hard to tell what this designation is meant to signify). A 300 SE of 1961 is accompanied by a 300 SEL 6·3 of 1967/72, a 450 SE of 1972/80, and one of the latest S Class range first seen at the 1979 Frankfurt Show

industry, that figure being lower than for any other production car.

As for the weight reduction achieved, the difficulty is to decide what new model should be compared with which of its predecessors. Daimler-Benz said the old 350 SE/SEL was being replaced by the new 280 SE/SEL, not the new 3·8-litre—which, they stated, was in fact the replacement for the 4·5-litre. Likewise, the 500 SE/SEL was not the successor to the old 450 SE/SEL, but to the former top-of-the-line model, the 450 SEL 6·9. Now the quoted kerb weight of the new 380 SE saloon, for example, was 176 lb below the old 350 SE's weight, but the slimming process seems *more* impressive if you compare it with the 450 SE, which was a full 374 lb heavier than the new 380 SE. Again, the new 500 SEL was said to scale 3641 lb—a hefty 616 lb less than the kerb weight of the 450 SEL 6·9.

And indeed, the performance figures given for the New S Class seemed to justify almost entirely this basis for comparison. In acceleration and maximum speed, the 3·8-litre models certainly looked like being a match for the previous 4·5-litres, with the new 5·0-litres well ahead of the latter, and apparently within striking distance of the superseded 6·9 also. As for fuel consumption, the claim was that a ten to twelve per cent improvement had been achieved across the board.

The wheelbases of the 3·8 and 5·0-litre models differed, as they had different back axles, but in the case of both the SE and SEL saloons they were slightly increased to reduce pitching. The bodyshells, too, were lengthened a little, the 380/500 SE being almost 1·5 inches longer than the 350/450 SE, and the 380/500 SEL nearly three inches more than the 350/450 SEL. All the new cars were almost two inches narrower than their predecessors, but there was no sacrifice of shoulder-room inside, and fore-and-aft space for the occupants was slightly increased. The cars were higher than their predecessors by varying amounts, depending on the model, but the amount

Daimler-Benz technicians work on a clay model of the new bodyshell, for which a fourteen per cent reduction in aerodynamic drag is claimed compared to its immediate predecessor

Here, a model of the new SEL can be compared with an actual SE in the metal. Only the wider rear door reveals the 140 mm difference in wheelbase between the two. In the SEL models, the extra length is used solely to increase space and legroom for the rear-seat passengers

was imperceptible. Crash resistance was further improved with a redesign of the front crush zone and windscreen pillars, and the doors were hung in such a way that jamming in an accident became less likely. Use of a more rigid steel plate (rustproofed at the more vulnerable areas) helped cut down weight while retaining body stability. Protective polyurethane foam-covered sidestrips were added, and the bumpers were of aluminium covered with the same material.

To satisfy new European regulations due in

April 1980, much was done to reduce external wind noise, which paid dividends for the occupants, also. Road noise, too, was reduced by using more rubber in the rear suspension, and as light-alloy engines are notoriously difficult to keep quiet, a double bulkhead was placed between engine and passenger compartments. Body seaming was also redesigned, with a view to cutting repair and part-repaint costs.

The interior was thoroughly worked over— starting with larger door-openings—to counter most of the rather niggling criticisms that some testers had been heard to make in the past. The

With their latest range of cars, Mercedes-Benz have become noticeably less Teutonic in their approach to interior design: this could be almost any Continental saloon instead of being Mercedes through and through

In some ways reminiscent of the 'New Generation' models that appeared more than a decade ago, the latest cars are so cleverly styled that, like this 500 SE, they look lower than the 450 SE and its sister cars although they are actually a fraction higher than before

seats, for instance (electrically adjusted, front and rear), were reshaped, and the front ones altered to allow more legroom for passengers in the back. There was a completely new heating and ventilating system that extracted stale air through the rear wheel-arches instead of the rear pillars. Bottom door-seals were improved. To make the front seat-belts safer and more comfortable, a choice of three top anchorages was provided, and the option of belt pre-tensioning was promised for the near future. Another promised option was a steering-wheel airbag which would inflate automatically in thirty milliseconds when deceleration reached a predetermined level; meanwhile the mechanical collapse of the

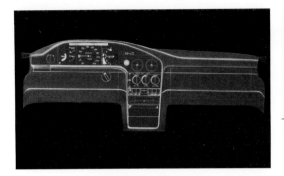
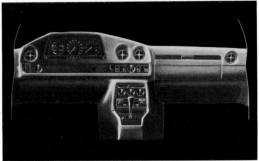

steering assembly was redesigned for greater safety, and the wheel slightly dished. In response to popular demand the wheel diameter was reduced—but only by a token 10 mm. The power-assisted steering, though already almost perfection, was made still better with detail modifications to the front suspension.

On the longer-wheelbase V8s, models 380/500 SEL, the hydro-pneumatic suspension developed for the 450 SEL 6·9 was offered as an option. Also available on the New S Class cars (as it had been on the previous New S Class models from late 1978) was Daimler-Benz's ABS (*Anti-Blockier-System*), which prevents wheel-lock under braking, thus allowing a driver to steer while applying

Two experimental facia layouts and the final choice adopted for the latest Mercedes range. 'A car is not an aeroplane', say Daimler-Benz, who believe that instruments and controls should be arranged with functional simplicity

full braking power, even on slush or snow. A similar system, intended for Mercedes commercial vehicles, is at present being developed in association with the American Westinghouse subsidiary at Hanover.

Much of the weight-saving in the new Series 126 bodyshell would have been impossible had it not been designed around a lighter engine than the existing range of cast-iron V8s: 3·5-, 4·5-, 6·3- and 6·9-litre. However, the light-alloy V8 was not completely new to us, for Daimler-Benz had as usual performed some of their development work in public. Just as the 3·5-litre V8 had first been tried out in an existing coupé that was somewhat long in the tooth, the new lightweight V8 first appeared at the 1977 Frankfurt Show under the bonnet of a much-lightened 450 SLC—not even a

At Sindelfingen, new production facilities have been arranged for the latest models to boost output to almost half-a-million cars a year. This rollover jig is a considerable aid to assembly work

245 kg

200 kg

member of the previous S Class, since that car belonged to the aging Series 107 like its ancestor, the original 350 SL roadster. But the engine was then in 5-litre guise, and when Paul Frère tested the coupé at Hockenheim he expressed delight, saying he found the handling surprisingly good (considering that the front suspension had by then been outdated by the zero-offset layout of the Series 116 S Class cars). In a more extended test for

Several different figures have been quoted by Daimler-Benz for the weight reductions achieved with the latest light-alloy V8 engines. Certainly the new 5-litre is appreciably lighter than the cast-iron 6·9, and the 3·8-litre weighs far less than the previous 4·5

105

Motor in 1978, he succeeded in *averaging* 100 mph when going from Paris to Nice, a distance of 580 miles, and classed the re-engined coupé as Mercedes-Benz's answer to the Porsche 928. The following year, one of these 5-litre cars finished second in that very demanding rally, the East African Safari, and there were the usual hopeful rumours of a full-scale return to competitions. Instead, the 450 SLC 5·0, as it was called in accordance with the confused nomenclature of the period, was simply offered for sale in Germany. More recently it has also been marketed in other parts of Europe, but it has not so far been available in Britain or America.

In designing the new engine, Daimler-Benz had naturally started with the V8s already in production, then set about lightening them and achieving still better bottom-end torque without loss of smooth running. Like the sump and cylinder heads, the block was now made in light alloy: a low-pressure casting made in a steel mould. Following a system already successfully by Porsche and Chevrolet for some of their models (and tried out by Mercedes in the Wankel-engined C.111), it was chemically treated to expose silicon crystals in the cylinder walls, giving a good wearing surface without any of the problems associated with steel liners. The pistons were iron-plated by some Daimler-Benz suppliers, and soft-chromed by others. Valve stems were hard-chromed for longer life, and the excellent hydraulic-fulcrum rocker arms of the cast-iron engines were retained. So was the K-Jetronic injection system, except that it, too, was now made in light alloy. Altogether, engine weights were reduced by 114 and 295 lb respectively, comparing the 5·0- with the 6·9-litre, and the 3·8- with the 4·5-litre. To those who remarked that a light-alloy engine cost more energy to produce

As before, there is little other than the badge to distinguish one Mercedes model from another in the same range. These three short-wheelbase models are the 500 SE V8, the 380 SE V8, and the six-cylinder 280 SE

than its cast-iron equivalent, Professor Breitschwerdt answered that the break-even point was 100,000 km, or about four years' use in an S class Mercedes-Benz.

Maximum power output was 218 bhp at 5500 rpm for the new V8 in its 3818 cc ($92 \times 71{\cdot}8$ mm) form, and 240 bhp at 4750 rpm as a 4973 cc ($96{\cdot}5 \times 85$ mm) unit. The maximum torque figures were respectively 220 lb ft at 4000 rpm, and 292 lb ft at 3200. So there was a marked improvement over the 3·5- and 4·5-litre cast-iron units, but it would be wishful thinking to suggest that the 3·8-litre engine gave a better output than the 4·5, or the 5·0-litre than the 6·9. Comparing car for car as Mercedes advised, reduced overall weight and body drag also came into the picture.

The other big change revealed by the Frankfurt Show of 1979 lay in the automatic transmission. In the 450 SLC 5·0 coupé, the three-speed torque converter system developed for the 4·5-litre was

Professor Hans-Joachim Förster, head of the automatic transmission department, is also the Director in charge of long-term development. It was under his guidance that Daimler-Benz designed the latest four-speed for use with the new light-alloy V8 engines

used (it still is, at the time of writing, but now is scheduled to be changed). With fuel economy primarily in mind, Daimler-Benz turned to a new four-speed torque converter system which, they said, was equal in performance to a five-speed manual gearbox, and reduced transmission losses by one-third. According to Stuttgart, an overdrive or a five-speed manual box with high top gear did not provide real fuel economy, because in practice a driver seldom bothered to engage overdrive, and usually changed down when overtaking. Therefore, they claimed, it was better to have a transmission system that would automatically hang onto the higher ratios, changing down only at a comparatively wide throttle opening (but without kickdown). This not only made for economy, but also encouraged smoothness.

For myself, driving the new cars in Germany towards the end of 1979, I thought the arrangement much better suited to the 5·0- than the 3·8-litre, which, with less bottom-end torque available, seemed to need a very heavy right foot when overtaking slower vehicles. When I raised this with Professor H-M. Förster, who is head of the Daimler-Benz automatic transmission division and also Director of long-term development, he agreed that some drivers prefer a fast response for quick, safe overtaking, while others value a very smooth change above all else. The characteristics of the new transmission might, he said, be modified somewhat before the New S Class went into full-scale production.

For that, the target date was March 1980, when it was hoped that production of the light-alloy V8 engines would have increased sufficiently to meet the demands of the new assembly plant that Daimler-Benz have built at Sindelfingen, fourteen kilometers from Stuttgart-Untertürkheim, as part of their ten billion Deutschemark investment

programme for the future. By that time the 350 SE/SEL, 450 SE/SEL and 450 SEL 6·9 saloons would be no more, their place having been taken by the new models, but there are apparently no plans to build a replacement for the old Series 107 roadster and coupé bodyshell of the 350 SL/SLC, 450 SL/SLC and 450 SLC 5·0—still selling, all of them, and especially in the USA, where two-thirds of total roadster/coupé production is exported.

On the latest S Class cars the lower body panels, front and rear, are made in polyurethane so that they may flex slightly if nudged in parking, and there are polyurethane sidestrips as well. Clean lines are enhanced by the way the wipers park out of sight

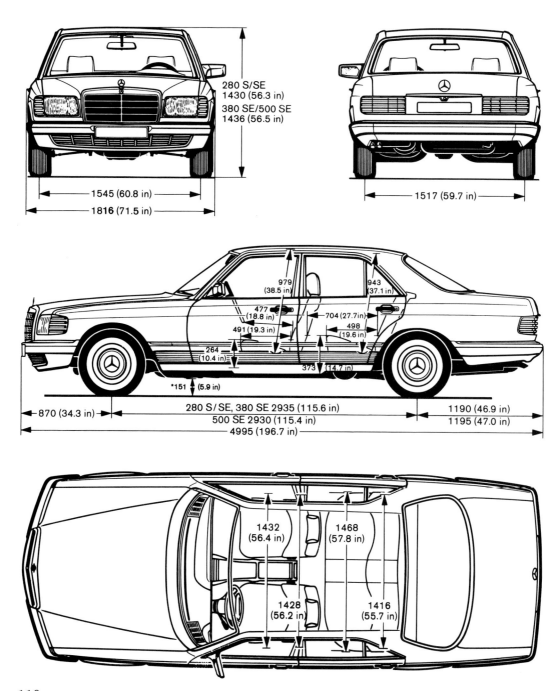

280 S/SE
1430 (56.3 in)
380 SE/500 SE
1436 (56.5 in)

1545 (60.8 in)
1816 (71.5 in)

1517 (59.7 in)

979
(38.5 in)
943
(37.1 in)
477
(18.8 in)
704 (27.7 in)
491 (19.3 in)
498
(19.6 in)
264
(10.4 in)
373 (14.7 in)
*151 (5.9 in)

870 (34.3 in)
280 S/SE, 380 SE 2935 (115.6 in)
500 SE 2930 (115.4 in)
4995 (196.7 in)
1190 (46.9 in)
1195 (47.0 in)

1432
(56.4 in)
1468
(57.8 in)
1428
(56.2 in)
1416
(55.7 in)

And of necessity the cast-iron V8 engines continue in production until 1 September 1981, the start of the first available New Model Year when the light-alloy engines could be introduced to America—or, indeed, to Australia.

Even before full production began, however, prices for the new V8 saloons on the domestic market had been announced. With thirteen per cent tax, they were DM46,669 (£12,280) for the 380 SE, DM49,042 (£12,906) for the 380 SEL, DM50,680 (£13,337) for the 500 SE, and DM56,161 (£14,779) for the 500 SEL—sterling prices quoted at DM3·8/£1.

For Daimler-Benz, as for all motor manufacturers, the future is far from certain, but few are better placed to develop their vehicles in whatever direction seems best suited to the energy situation. Without abandoning their own standards, they have already put into production a range of light and low-drag cars that might still meet their customers' needs to the end of the present century. Their V8 engines have been so designed that, if necessary, torque can be maximized at even lower rpm. The first steps have already been taken to develop a 'cylinder cut-off' system, putting two or four cylinders out of action to reduce fuel consumption by as much as thirty per cent, and although Daimler-Benz are not alone in this work, they are in the fortunate position of knowing that V8 engines are well-suited to this scheme, mechanical balance being maintained throughout. As a final shot in their locker, they are also working on a V8 diesel engine and a gas turbine.

Professor Zahn, outgoing Chairman of the Board of Directors, promised that further development would continue along well-established lines, when he talked to the Press at the 1979 Frankfurt Show. 'We have no intention of enter-

Left All the latest S Class cars have the same tracks front or rear and the bodies are the same width, but there are minor differences in height. All short-wheelbase models are the same overall length, as are all long-wheelbase cars. The 3·8-litre and 5-litre models are of different wheelbases, however, because they have different rear axles

111

*Professor Joachim Zahn,
Chairman of the Daimler-
Benz board of management
until early 1980, put his faith
in the development of
existing Mercedes designs
rather than a radical change
of policy. Refusing to be
panicked by the energy crisis,
he declared with smiling
assurance, 'We believe that it
is perfectly possible to
continue building cars for
the discerning, while
fulfilling the need to save
energy'*

ing the market of mass-produced cars—as regards production figures, marketing and the quality of our cars, this would mean leaving the proven Daimler-Benz path. . . . It is not necessary for us to do a complete about-turn; it is perfectly possible to make cars for the discerning, and at the same time fulfil the need to save energy'.

Specifications

Type 600 (Series 100)

Production period	Late 1963 onwards (built to order only)
Body style(s)	Standard four-door six-light, Pullman four-door eight-light, Pullman six-door eight-light

Engine

Materials	Cast iron cylinder block/crankcase with light alloy heads
Configuration	V8 (90 deg)
Bore, stroke & capacity	103×95 mm = 6332 cc
Compression ratio	9·0 to 1
Max power	250 bhp net (187 Kw) at 4000 rpm
Max torque	369 lb ft net (51 mkg) at 2800 rpm
Valve gear	One ohc (chain-driven) per cylinder bank, with finger-type rockers
Induction system	Bosch fuel injection to inlet ports by 8-plunger pump. Electric feed pump from 24·7-gallon (112-litre) tank

Lubrication	Wet sump, 10·6 pints (6 litres) capacity. Two filters
Transmission	Mercedes-Benz type K4B 050 four-speed automatic with fluid coupling. Optional selector position
Overall ratios	12·87, 8·14, 5·10 and 3·23 to 1 (reverse, 13·4). Limited-slip differential
Top gear speed/1000 rpm	25·8 mph (41·5 km/h)
Chassis	
Front suspension	Wishbones on subframe with compressor-fed air units, auxiliary rubber springs and telescopic dampers. Anti-roll bar
Rear suspension	Single-low-pivot swing-axle with compressor-fed air units, auxiliary rubber springs and telescopic dampers. Ride softness and ground clearance adjustable by driver. Self-levelling
Steering	Daimler-Benz recirculating ball, power-assisted
Brakes	ATE disc, front and rear. Dual-circuit system with pneumatic servo and twin calipers at front

Tyres   900H-15 on 6·5 in rims

Equipment   Many variations due to
                           individual orders, but
                           normally includes two-
                           speed wipers,
                           screenwasher and
                           heated backlight fed by
                           12-volt Bosch system
                           with dual alternators.
                           Pneumatically-
                           operated window lifts,
                           seat adjustment,
                           centralized door
                           locking, bootlid
                           locking, etc. Optional
                           air-conditioning and
                           powered sunroof. Two-
                           level horn, adjustable
                           (from interior) outside
                           mirror and adjustable
                           steering column length

Dimensions
Wheelbase   126 in (3200 mm) *or*
                           153·5 in (3900 mm)
Track (front)   62·5 in (1590 mm)
Track (rear)   62·0 in (1570 mm)
Overall length   218 in (5540 mm) *or* 246
                           in (6250 mm)
Height   59·5 in (1510 mm)
Width   76·8 in (1950 mm)
Unladen weight   5445 lb (2470 kg) *or* 5820
                           lb (2640 kg)

Production   2613 cars to October
                           1979

Type 300 SEL 6·3 (Series 109)

Production period	Late 1967 to late 1972
Body style(s)	Four-door saloon, as contemporary six-cylinder model
Engine	As Type 600, but fuel tank 23·1 gall (105 litres)
Transmission	As Type 600, but overall ratios 11·34, 7·00, 4·50 and 2·85 to 1 (reverse, 11·82)
Top gear speed/1000 rpm	27·5 mph (44·25 km/h)
Chassis	Basically as Type 600, but ventilated-disc brakes all round with single calipers at front, and higher-geared steering
Tyres	700 × 14 high-speed radial on 6·5 in rims
Equipment	Simplified version of Model 600 specification, including pneumatically-operated window lifts, centralized door locking and bootlid locking, but excluding powered seat adjustment, etc
Dimensions	
Wheelbase	112·8 in (2865 mm)

Track (front)	58·4 in (1482 mm)
Track (rear)	58·7 in (1490 mm)
Overall length	196·9 in (5000 mm)
Height	55·5 in (1410 mm)
Width	71·3 in (1810 mm)
Unladen weight	3828 lb (1740 kg)
Production	6526 cars

Type 300 SEL 3·5 (Series 109)

Production period	Late 1969 to late 1972
Body style(s)	Four-door saloon, as 6-cyl and V8 6·3-litre versions

Engine

Materials	Cast iron cylinder block/crankcase, light alloy heads and sump
Configuration	V8 (90 deg)
Bore, stroke & capacity	92 × 65·8 mm = 3499 cc
Compression ratio	9·5 to 1
Max power	200 bhp net (147 Kw) at 5800 rpm
Max torque	211 lb ft net (29·2 mkg) at 4000 rpm
Valve gear	One ohc (chain-driven) per cylinder bank, with finger-type rockers (ball-joint mounted)
Induction system	Bosch fuel injection (D-Jetronic electronically controlled) to inlet ports
Lubrication	Wet sump, 11·5 pints (6·5 litres) capacity.

	Full-flow filter and oil-cooler
Ignition	Bosch transistorized
Transmission	Mercedes-Benz type K4A 040 four-speed automatic with fluid coupling, or four-speed manual. Selector on floor or steering column (optional)
Overall ratios	Automatic: 14·69, 8·82, 5·39 and 3·69 to 1 (reverse, 20·9). Manual: 14·18, 8·64, 5·31 and 3·69 to 1 (reverse, 13·71)
Top gear speed/1000 rpm	19·9 mph (32 km/h)
Chassis	Basically as 300 SEL 6·3, but tyres 185 × 14 on 6·5 in rims
Dimensions	As 300 SEL 6·3, but unladen weight 3680 lb (1670 kg)
Production	9583 cars (8518 automatic)

Types 280 SE and SEL 3·5 (Series 108)

Production period	Early 1971 to mid-1972 Neither car sold in USA. 280 SEL 3·5 not sold in UK
Body style(s)	Four-door saloons similar to 6-cyl models,

but some detail
modifications
according to market

Engine   As 300 SEL 3·5

Transmission   As 300 SEL 3·5

Chassis

Front suspension   Wishbones on subframe
with coil springs and
anti-roll bar

Rear suspension   Single-low-pivot swing-
axle with coil springs
and radius arms. Self-
levelling

Steering   Daimler-Benz
recirculating ball,
power-assisted

Brakes   ATE disc, front and
rear, power-assisted
and ventilated at front

Tyres   735H14/185H14

Dimensions

Wheelbase   110 in (2750 mm) *or*
112·2 in (2850 mm)

Track (front)   58·4 in (1482 mm)
Track (rear)   58·7 in (1490 mm)
Overall length   184 in (4680 mm) *or*
188 in (4780 mm)

Height   56·7 in (1440 mm)
Width   71·3 in (1810 mm)
Unladen weight   3800 lb (1727 kg) *or*
3880 lb (1764 kg)

Production   (280 SE 3·5) 11,309 cars
(8967 automatic)
(280 SEL 3·5) 951 cars
(745 automatic)

Types 280 SE and SEL 4·5 (Series 108)

Production period	Early 1971 to late 1972. Sold in USA only
Body style(s)	As 280 SE and SEL 3·5 saloons (US specification)
Engine	As in later (1973) 450 SEL saloon, but 8·1 to 1 compression ratio and 230 bhp (SAE) output for US market
Transmission	Automatic transmission only: Mercedes-Benz type W3A 040 three-speed with torque converter
Overall ratios	7·46, 4·72 and 3·23 to 1 (reverse, 5·94)
Top gear speed/1000 rpm	22·7 mph (36·5 km/h)
Chassis	As 280 SE and SEL 3·5
Dimensions	As 280 SE and SEL
Production	(280 SE 4·5) 13,527 cars (all automatic) (280 SEL 4·5) 8173 cars (all automatic)

Type 300 SEL 4·5 (Series 109)

Production period	Early 1971 to late 1972. Sold in USA only
Body style(s)	Four-door saloon, as

	other 300 SEL models
Engine	As in 280 SE and SEL 4·5 models
Transmission	As in 280 SE and SEL 4·5 models
Chassis	As 300 SEL 3·5 model
Production	2553 cars (all automatic)

Types 350 SE and SEL (Series 116)

Production period	(350 SE) 1972 to 1980. (350 SEL) 1973 to 1980. Not sold in UK
Body style(s)	Longer, lower New S-Class four-door saloons with crush sections front and rear, reinforced roof, four headlamps paired horizontally, etc
Engine	As in 300 SEL 3·5, but D-Jetronic injection system replaced by K-Jetronic (mechanically-controlled) and hydraulic rocker adjustment incorporated, January 1976. Later compression ratio, 9·0 to 1. Max power output later 195 bhp (143 Kw) at 5500 rpm. Max

torque later 202 lb ft (28 mkg) at 4000 rpm.

Transmission

Normally Mercedes-Benz type W3A 040 three-speed with torque converter, and option of column or floor-mounted selector. Four-speed manual listed as option

Overall ratios

(Automatic) 7·99, 5·05 and 3·46 to 1 (reverse, 6·37). (Manual) 13·7, 8·1, 4·95 and 3·46 to 1 (reverse, 12·87)

Top gear
speed/1000 rpm

21·3 mph (34·3 km/h)

Chassis

Front suspension

Anti-dive, zero-offset with double wishbones, coil springs, and forward location by anti-roll bar. Telescopic dampers, gas-filled

Rear suspension

Semi-trailing arm independent with coil springs and anti-roll bar. Telescopic dampers, gas-filled. Optional self-levelling control

Steering

Daimler-Benz recirculating ball, power-assisted, with telescopic damper

Brakes

ATE discs, front and

	rear (ventilated at front), with dual-circuit system and vacuum booster
Tyres	205/70HR14 on 6·5J rims
Equipment	Varies according to market (eg vacuum-operated central door-locking standard for UK cars). Normally includes electric window lifts, heated rear window, laminated windscreen, tinted glass, head restraints, seat-belts front and rear, childproof locks, warning triangle and first-aid kit, self-cleaning side and rear windows and tail-light clusters. Headlamp wash/wipe optional. Radio optional. Tachometer optional

Dimensions

Wheelbase	112·8 in (2865 mm) *or* 116·7 in (2965 mm)
Track (front)	59·9 in (1521 mm)
Track (rear)	59·3 in (1505 mm)
Overall length	195·3 in (4960 mm) *or* 199·2 in (5060 mm)
Height	56·1 in (1425 mm)
Width	73·6 in (1870 mm)
Unladen weight	3685 lb (1675 kg) *or* 3740 lb (1700 kg)

Production	350 SE: With D-Jetronic injection, 31,366 cars; with K-Jetronic, 19,269 cars to October 1979 350 SEL: With D-Jetronic injection, 1139 cars; with K-Jetronic, 3020 cars to October 1979

Type 450 SE and SEL (Series 116)

Production period	1972 to 1980
Body style(s)	Identical to 350 SE and SEL but for minor details of equipment (see below)

Engine

Materials	Cast iron cylinder block/crankcase, light alloy heads and sump
Configuration	V8 (90 deg)
Bore, stroke & capacity	92 × 85 mm = 4520 cc
Compression ratio	8·8 to 1 (8·1 in USA)
Max power	Varies according to emission-control equipment, etc. Earlier European specification units, 225 bhp (168 Kw) at 5000 rpm; later, 217 bhp (160Kw). USA specification, 190 bhp SAE at 4750 rpm (California, 180 bhp)
Max torque	Varies as above. Earlier European specification units,

	278 lb ft (38·4 mkg) at 3000 rpm; later, 265·5 lb ft (36·7 mkg). USA specification, 238·7 lb ft (California, 232 lb ft)
Valve gear	One ohc (chain-driven) per cylinder bank, with finger-type rockers (hydraulically adjusted from October 1975)
Induction system	Bosch fuel injection to inlet ports (D-Jetronic electronically controlled replaced by K-Jetronic mechanically controlled system in October 1975)
Lubrication	Wet sump, 11·5 pints (6·5 litres) capacity
Ignition	Bosch transistorized (contactless)
Transmission	Automatic only, but optional Tempomat cruise control. European cars, Daimler-Benz type W3B 050 three-speed automatic with torque converter. US cars, type W3A 040 (as in automatic 350 SE and SEL models, but final drive 3·07 instead of 3·46 to 1)
Overall ratios	(European and USA) 7·09, 4·48 and 3·07 to 1

	(reverse, 5·65)
Top gear speed/1000 rpm	24·0 mph (38·6 km/h)
Chassis	Basically as 350 SE and SEL but fractionally shorter wheelbase, starting torque compensator incorporated. Tyres 205/70VR14
Equipment	Varies according to market. Basically as 350 SE and SEL but headlamp wash/wipe standardized, head restraints front and rear
Dimensions	As 350 SE and SEL, except as below:
Wheelbase	112·6 in (2860 mm) *or* 116·5 (2960 mm)
Weight	3883 lb (1765 kg) *or* 3938 lb (1790 kg)
Production	450 SE: With D-Jetronic injection, 25,703 cars; with K-Jetronic, 16,463 cars to October 1979 450 SEL: With D-Jetronic injection, 21,471 cars; with K-Jetronic, 36,453 cars to October 1979

Type 450 SEL 6·9 (Series 116)

Production period	Mid-1975 to late 1979
Body style	Identical to 450 SEL four-door saloon

Engine

Materials	Cast iron cylinder block/crankcase with light alloy heads. Reinz-Repa head gaskets
Configuration	V8 (90 deg)
Bore, stroke & capacity	107×95 mm $= 6834$ cc
Compression ratio	8·8 to 1
Max power	286 bhp DIN (210 Kw) at 4250 rpm
Max torque	405 lb ft (56 mkg) at 3000 rpm
Valve gear	One ohc (chain-driven) per cylinder bank, with hydraulically adjusted finger-type rockers
Induction system	Bosch K-Jetronic (mechanically controlled) fuel injection to inlet ports
Lubrication	Dry sump, total capacity 21 pints (12 litres)
Ignition	Bosch transistorized (contactless)

Transmission   Automatic only, with Tempomat cruise control. Daimler-Benz type W3B 050 three-speed automatic with torque converter, as on

	smaller-engined 450 SE and SEL models, but with 2·65 to 1 final drive. Limited-slip differential
Overall ratios	6·12, 3·87 and 2·65 to 1 (reverse, 4·88)
Top gear speed/1000 rpm	28·4 mph (45·7 km/h)

Chassis

Suspension	Oleo-gas self-levelling system with anti-dive front and anti-squat rear controls, plus adjustable ground clearance
Steering	As 350/450/SE/SEL
Brakes	As 350/450/SE/SEL, with stepped master cylinder
Tyres	215/70VR14 on light alloy wheels

Equipment	Varies according to market, but normally as smaller-engined 450 SEL model plus standardized air conditioning and tachometer
Dimensions	As 450 SEL but Height=55·5 in (1410 mm) and Weight=4257 lb (1935 kg)
Production	6988 cars

Types 380 SE and SEL (Series 126)

Production period	From 1980 onwards
Body style(s)	Redesigned, lower-drag 'new New S-Class' four-door saloons, longer and narrower with pointed nose and full-length polyurethane side bumpers along bottom edge of body

Engine

Materials	All-alloy block/crankcase, heads and sump with siliconized cylinder bores and iron-plated or soft-chromed pistons. Light-alloy injection system
Configuration	V8 (90 deg)
Bore, stroke & capacity	$92 \times 71 \cdot 8$ mm $= 3818$ cc
Compression ratio	9·0 to 1
Max power	218 bhp DIN (160 Kw) at 5500 rpm
Max torque	221 lb ft (305 Nm) at 4000 rpm
Valve gear	One ohc (chain-driven) per cylinder bank, with hydraulically-adjusted finger-type rockers
Induction sytem	Bosch K-Jetronic injection to inlet ports
Lubrication	Wet sump with external filter. Total capacity, 14 pints (8 litres)
Ignition	Bosch transistorized (contactless)

Transmission	Daimler-Benz type W4A 040 four-speed automatic transmission with torque converter
Overall ratios	12·03, 7·88, 4·71 and 3·27 to 1 (reverse, 16·81)
Top gear speed/1000 rpm	22·04 mph (35·46 km/h)

Chassis

Front suspension	Anti-dive, zero-offset with double wishbones, coil springs, and forward location by anti-roll bar. Telescopic dampers, gas-filled
Rear suspension	Semi-trailing arm independent with coil springs and anti-roll bar. Telescopic dampers, gas-filled.
Optional suspension	Oleo-gas self-levelling system available on 380 SEL
Steering	Daimler-Benz power-assisted, with telescopic damper
Brakes	ATE discs, front and rear (ventilated at front), with dual-circuit system and vacuum booster. Stepped master cylinder. Optional anti-lock braking system
Tyres	205/70VR14 on 6·5J × 14 H2 wheels

| Equipment | Varies according to market. New items include electronically-controlled heating unit (with option of air-conditioning), electrically-operated seat adjustment, electrically-adjusted exterior mirror, three-way adjustment of seat-belt guide, and facia 'Econometer' |

Dimensions

Wheelbase	115·6 in (2935 mm) *or* 121·1 in (3075 mm)
Track (front)	60·8 in (1545 mm)
Track (rear)	59·7 in (1517 mm)
Overall length	196·7 in (4995 mm) *or* 202·2 (5135 mm)
Height	56·5 in (1436 mm) *or* 56·7 (1440 mm)
Width	71·5 in (1816 mm)
Unladen weight	3509 lb (1595 kg) *or* 3553 lb (1615 kg)

| **Production** | Current models |

Types 500 SE and SEL (Series 126)

| Production period | From 1980 onwards |
| Body style(s) | As 380 SE and SEL |

Engine

| Materials and configuration | As 380 SE and SEL |
| Bore, stroke & capacity | 96·5 × 85 mm = 4973 cc |

131

Compression ratio	8·8 to 1
Max power	240 bhp DIN (177 Kw) at 4750 rpm
Max torque	292 lb ft (404 Nm) at 3200 rpm
Valve gear	As 380 SE and SEL
Induction system	As 380 SE and SEL
Lubrication	As 380 SE and SEL
Ignition	As 380 SE and SEL

Transmission   As 380 SE and SEL, but with 2·82 to 1 final drive

Overall ratios	10·38, 6·8, 4·06 and 2·82 to 1 (reverse, 14·5)
Top gear speed/1000 rpm	25·63 mph (41·24 km/h)

Chassis

Suspension	As 380 SE and SEL Oleo-gas self-levelling system available on 500 SEL as option
Steering	As 380 SE and SEL
Brakes	As 380 SE and SEL
Tyres	As 380 SE and SEL

Equipment   As 380 SE and SEL

Dimensions

Wheelbase	115·4 in (2930 mm) *or* 120·9 in (3070 mm)
Tracks, front and rear	As 380 SE and SEL
Overall length	As 380 SE *or* as 380 SEL
Height	As 380 SE *or* as 380 SEL
Width	As 380/SE and SEL
Unladen weight	3564 lb (1620 kg) *or* 3641 lb (1655 kg)

Production   Current models

Photographic Acknowledgements

No one not involved in book production will appreciate how much the publisher relies upon a car manufacturer. Without their help, if not in supplying pictorial material then in aiding its analysis, we would be lost.

Both the public relations and photographic personnel at Daimler-Benz AG in Stuttgart in West Germany and at Mercedes-Benz (United Kingdom) Ltd provided many photographs and much help without more than an 'of course'. And to our 'yesterday?' they replied 'tomorrow' and it arrived. Thank you.

Other illustrative help came from Mrs Eileen Brockbank, Mirco Decet, Jean-Francois Marchet, the author and Mrs Caroline Nostrand McComb, Tim Parker Collection, H. P. Seufert, Jeremy Walton and Nicky Wright. A number of Mercedes owners polished their cars on our behalf and the kind proprietor of Chicheley Hall, near Newport Pagnell, offered his grounds to the author as a suitable backdrop for the colour shot of the 6·9 litre 450 SEL. Thank you all.

Index

A
Alfa Romeo P3 **21**
American Westinghouse **104**
Aston Martin V8 **93**
ATE **114, 119, 122, 130**
Austin Allegro **25**
Austro Daimler **25**
Auto Union **22**
Avusrennen **10**

B
Bendix **58**
Benz, Karl **12**
Benz Tropfenwagen **17**
Bismark **9**
BMW **57**
Boddy, Bill **43**
Bosch **24, 39, 58, 83, 113, 115, 118, 125, 129**
Brands Hatch **49**
Breitschwerdt, Professor Werner **96, 106**
Bruce-Brown **14**
Bugatti Type 35B **21**
Burman, Bob **15**

C
Cadillac **95**
Cadillac Fleetwood **75**
        Imperial **34**
California **11**
Cannstatt Daimler **12**

Caracciola, Rudi **9, 10, 21, 26, 27, 28, 29**
Chevrolet **106**
Chevrolet Corvette Sting Ray **52**

D
Daimler-Benz **16**
Daimler-Benz AG **8, 12, 19, 30, 55**
Daimler Company **13, 14**
Daimler Phoenix 24 hp **12**
Daimler, Gottlieb **12**
Daytona Beach **14**
De Caters, Baron **14**
Dieppe **14**

E
East African Safari **106**
Eifelrennen **10**
Eliot, T. S. **10**
Engel, Werner **32**
European Car of the Year committee **81**

F
Fangio, Juan Manuel **32**
Ferrari **54**
Ford Mercury **9**
Förster, Professor Hans-Joachim **108**
Frankfurt **82**
Frankfurt Show **96, 98, 104, 107, 112**

French Grand Prix **14, 15**
Frère, Paul **43, 54, 80**
Frogeye Sprite **8**

G
General Motors **34**
Geneva Show **49, 76, 84**
German Grand Prix **10, 16**
Gordon Bennet Trophy **14**
Guinness, Sir Alec **93**

H
Hanover **104**
Hémery, Victor **15**
Herrmann, Hans **51**
Hitler, Adolf **19, 20, 21**
Hockenheim **26, 105**

I
Ickx, Jackie **51**
Italian Grand Prix **22**

J
Jaguar **9**
Jaguar V12 E type **91**
        XJ 5·3 **93**
        XJ 12 **80**
Jellinek, Emile **12, 13, 14**
Jellinek, Mercédès **13**

L
Laguna Seca **50**
Lamborghini **54**
Lang **9, 26, 27, 28**

La Rue, Danny 93
La Turbie hillclimb 92
Lautenschlager 15
Libya 28
Ludvigsen, Karl 15

M
Macao Six Hours 51, 54
Mannheim 15
Maserati 21
Maserati Khamsin 91
Maybach, Wilhelm 12
Mercedes-Benz
   200 17
   220 17
   230 17, 48
   250 17, 56
   280 56
   280 S 64
   280 SE 60, 63, 98, 107
   280 SEL 60, 62, 63, 64, 98
   300 17, 30
   300 SE 38, 39, 98
   300 SEL 49, 50, 52, 58, 59,
     60, 64, 76, 84, 89, 121
   350 SL 61, 62, 73, 75, 81,
     105, 109
   350 SLC 61, 62, 73, 75, 82,
     109
   350 SL 4·5 63
   450 SL 76, 81, 109
   450 SLC 76, 82, 104, 109
   450 SLC 5·0 106, 107, 109
   500K 10, 11, 18
   540K 10, 11, 49
   21 litre Blitzen Benz 15
   Grosser 18, 19, 20, 32, 34,
     36, 37, 39, 47, 86, 93, 95
   C.111 75, 106
   M.154 23
   M.165 24, 25
   Series 100 113
   Series 107 61, 105, 109
   Series 108 118, 120
   Series 109 57, 59, 116, 117,
     120
   Series 111 60
   Series 114/115 57, 61, 75

   Series 116 64, 79, 85, 89,
     96, 105, 121, 124, 127
   Series 126 96, 104, 111,
     129, 131
   SSK 18, 21
   SSKL 9, 10, 49
   W.154 22, 25
   W.165 20, 22, 26, 28, 29
   W.196 29
   ZF 25, 94
Mercedes-Benz Roadsters 64
Mille Miglia 10
Mini 50
Monthoux 49
Monza 22
Moscow 14
Motor 47, 48, 73, 76, 79, 81,
   88, 91, 105
Motor Sport 29, 43, 47, 79
Motor, The 20
Munich 82
Mussolini, Benito 21, 28

O
Oldfield, Barney 14
OPEC 49

P
Panhard & Levassor 13
Paris 106
Paris Salon 64
Pau Grand Prix 26
Porsche 54, 106
Porsche 928 106

R
Reinz-Repa 87
Road & Track 30, 32, 52, 54,
   61, 79, 81, 91
Rolls-Royce 95
Rolls-Royce
   Phantom V 34
   Silver Cloud II 38
   Silver Shadow 81
   Silver Shadow II 91, 93

S
Scherenberg, Professor Dr
   Hans 88

Sedgwick, Stanley 47
Setright, L. J. K. 64
Sindelfingen 104, 107
Spa 24 Hours 51, 54
St. Petersburg 14
Stuttgart 11, 12, 16, 20, 25,
   26, 29, 32, 55, 57, 75, 79, 84,
   89, 91, 95, 96, 107
Stuttgart-Unterturkheim 22,
   108

T
Tripoli 24, 29
Tripoli Grand Prix 22, 23,
   26, 27, 28, 37

U
Uhlehaut, Rudolf 50

V
Vanderbilt, William K. 14
Volkswagen 58
Von Brauchitsch 9

W
Waxenberger, Erich 51, 54
Werner 92

Z
Zahn, Professor Joachim
   111, 112